Beat the builders at their games of l
trump card for the householder . . .

Sunday Times

Is your time worth the money? . . . The *Home Improvement Price Guide* gives specific information about how much, in terms of materials and labour, repairs and improvements will cost . . . clear and easy to understand format . . .

The Guardian

. . . packed with technically and professionally accurate information, while still retaining a writing style that is straightforward and should be easy for the layperson to understand.

The Star Property Weekly

It charts how long it should take to do each job, what degree of skill is needed, what amounts of materials are required and how much it should cost the DIY enthusiast compared with the professional.

The Observer

. . . the first manual of costs in the building trade, designed specifically for the man who needs it most: the customer, who's paying the bill.

The Liverpool Daily Post

HOME *Improvement* PRICE GUIDE

Second edition

Bryan J.D. Spain
FInstCES, MACostE

and

Leonard B. Morley
DipQS, FRICS, MInstCES, MACostE

LONDON
E. & F.N. SPON

First published in 1987 by
E. & F.N. Spon Ltd
11 New Fetter Lane, London EC4P 4EE

Reprinted 1987, 1988
Second edition 1989

Printed in Great Britain by
T.J. Press Ltd, Padstow, Cornwall

ISBN 0 419 14900 7

British Library Cataloguing in Publication Data

Spain, Bryan J.D.
Home improvement price guide. – 2nd ed
1. Residences. Building projects. Prices
I. Title II. Morley, Leonard B.
643'.7

ISBN 0-419-14900-7

Contents

Preface

Anyone who is responsible for house repairs and improvements should find this book a valuable source of information.

If you have neither the skill nor the desire to become involved in DIY work you will be able to judge whether you are paying the correct amount for a wide range of construction activities varying from replacing a broken pane of glass to building an extension.

Alternatively you may be the type who wishes to carry out yourself some or all of the multitude of jobs necessary to keep your property in good condition. In this case you will find useful information on the cost of materials and the length of time each job should take.

The descriptions of work have generally been arranged in elements rather than trades. In other words, locational headings are used, e.g. bathroom, kitchen, patio, regardless of the different trades or skills involved.

Most of the information in Chapter 4 is laid out in tables and the symbols used have the following meaning:

Description	Quantity	Total DIY hrs mins	Total DIY material £	Skill level	Contractor's price £

Description

This column describes the work to be carried out, and there are two main types:

(*a*) a complete operation usually involving only one trade or skill, e.g. replacing a broken roof tile;

(*b*) a cost per unit of an item, e.g. the cost per square yard or metre of laying a 100 mm thick concrete drive.

You should note that unless specifically mentioned the cost of removing debris is not included. Where possible the descriptions have been expressed in non-technical terms. The Glossary (p.189) defines the less common terms.

Quantity

The number, length, area or volume of the work described.

Total DIY hours

The time taken for carrying out each individual operation is expressed in hours and minutes – 2:15 therefore means 2 hours 15 minutes.

These hours show the number of hours likely to be taken by the average DIY enthusiast. The word 'average' is important in this context and should be taken as someone who has a basic knowledge of the use of tools together with an interest and enthusiasm for the work. An assessment of the total number of hours likely to be needed for each task is based upon average performances. The householder who works to a finish which could be described as 'acceptable' will obviously not take as long to complete the operation as a perfectionist who is looking for, say, a mirror finish on the paintwork. The hours, therefore, represent the time that should be taken by the average person in average conditions to produce an average finish. If two people were involved the allocation of hours shown should be halved. The time taken to prepare for work, moving furniture, taking up carpets and clearing away at the end of the work session has not been allowed for. All the hours stated assume that you can reach the work comfortably. If you have to use ladders or work in a confined space an extra 20% to 30% should be added.

Total DIY material

The cost of all materials has been based on the average prices for small and large quantities in DIY shops including VAT. An allowance has been made for waste but nothing has been included for the cost of transporting the materials from the shop to the home. Materials which are delivered are assumed to be deposited within a reasonable distance of the place of use and no allowance has been made in money or hours for their removal beyond that point. Assuming that the level of material prices in this book is 100, the following represents the costs in each region.

Scotland	–	96
Wales	–	98
Northern Ireland	–	91

England		
South West	–	94
South East	–	109
Home Counties	–	110
Inner London	–	130
Outer London	–	120
East Anglia	–	110
Midlands	–	102
North West	–	101
North East	–	96

If you live in the South West of England, therefore, the materials cost in this book should be reduced by 6%. Conversely, someone living in the South East should increase the costs by 9%.

Skill level

Each operation has been awarded a 'skill factor' ranging from 1 to 10 indicating the degree of difficulty likely to be encountered by the average DIYer. For example, scraping off wallpaper is given a rating of 1 – the simplest of tasks – but plastering is rated at 8. Generally speaking, jobs which have rating of 8, 9 or 10 should not be attempted by amateurs unless you are particularly gifted or can ask for experienced and professional help. This applies not only to obvious examples like electrical work but also to breaking out large openings or indeed to most work involving structural alterations.

Contractor's price

The total costs of the contractor's charges are included here. There is one important qualification which you must remember. Replacing a tap washer may only take a plumber a matter of minutes but you cannot expect his charges to be based solely on the time taken to do the work if that was the only task he was asked to carry out. He will also charge you for the cost of travelling but these hours and costs are not shown in this book.

The question of emergency call out charges must also be considered. A tradesman who responds to an emergency call will almost certainly be looking for a 'disturbance payment' in addition to the cost of his labour and materials. This should be discussed and agreed before the work is carried out to avoid misunderstandings.

It is a mistake to believe that a call out charge is only applicable outside normal working hours. An emergency call during the day can have a disruptive effect on the normal work pattern and should be paid for.

Some suggested levels of charges are set out below, but they should be regarded as only giving an indication:

Call out charge during working hours	£15-£20
Call out charge 6 pm to midnight	£20-£30
Call out charge after midnight, Sundays and Bank Holiday's	£30-£50

Other points to note

Chapter 2 deals with the problems of building regulations and planning procedures and when it is necessary to appoint an architect. The difference between estimates and quotations is explained and sensible procedures are listed for dealing with the acceptance of quotations, when and how much to pay and also with the vexed question of variations and extras. Chapter 6 gives general information on the approximate cost of domestic construction work.

You should bear in mind that the true cost of employing a contractor is not what you *ought* to be charged but what you *are* charged. For example, if there is a glut of work for painting contractors at one particular time, the prices they quote will exceed their normal charges because they have less need to be competitive. The opposite is also true, of course, and these factors can directly affect the costs. There are three main types of builders who carry out domestic repair, improvements and maintenance work:

(*a*) the small firm which has a manned office and is registered for VAT;
(*b*) a one man firm working from home;
(*c*) the tradesman who has full time employment but undertakes small jobs outside his normal working day.

In this book we have assumed that firm (a) above will be carrying out the work and VAT has been included in the Contractor's price column. This means that 15% for VAT will be included in your bill which, in most cases, you cannot reclaim.

Measurements in this book are given in both imperial and metric and the following abbreviations are used:

no	=	number	mm	=	millimetre
yd	=	yard	m	=	metre
sq yd	=	square yard	sq m	=	square metre
cu yd	=	cubic yard	cu m	=	cubic metre

The inclusion of both imperial and metric dimensions is intended to help you if you are unfamiliar with either form. Sometimes a metric (or imperial) equivalent has been given even though it is not possible to buy the material in that size. For example, all timber is sold in metric sizes nowadays but most DIY enthusiasts still think in 4″ × 2″ terms for a piece of timber which is 102 × 51 mm nominal size. This would appear in the book as 100 × 50 mm. Generally, however the materials are described in the sizes as they are sold.

There are now many women working as contractors. The pronoun 'he' used in this book applies to both men and women.

While every effort is made to ensure the accuracy of the information given in this publication, neither the authors nor the publishers accept liability of any kind resulting from the use made by any person of such information.

The authors would welcome constructive comments on the scope and contents with a view to improvement.

The authors have received much help from many individuals and firms in the preparation of this book and would like to make the following acknowledgements:

Federation of Master Builders
Paint and Painting Industries Liaison Committee
Crosby Doors Ltd
W.F. Hollway and Bros Ltd
John Carr Joinery Sales Ltd
Woodfit Ltd
Hire Service Shops Ltd
Banbury Homes and Gardens Ltd
Penguin Swimming Pools
Spike Boydell
Insight Marketing Services Ltd
John Thirlwell
Andy Williamson
Dorothy Spain
Russell Flynn
Susan Westcott

BRYAN J.D. SPAIN
and
LEONARD B. MORLEY
Spain and Partners
Consulting Quantity Surveyors
Unit 9
SMM Business Park
Dock Road, Birkenhead
Merseyside L41 1DT

BUILDING ESTIMATE
BUILDER
HOUSE EXTENSION
KENNEL

1 Using a contractor

When to use a contractor

Apart from buying a house or car, your largest expenditure will probably be having major home improvements carried out. With such a large expenditure, you will obviously want the finished job to be of a good standard. There are many projects when do-it-yourself skills will be insufficient for the work involved and a contractor must be used.

If you are not interested in DIY at all then you will be totally dependent upon contractors for your repairs and improvements. But even if you have only a moderate level of do-it-yourself skills you may have several options on how to carry out any particular job.

Take as an example a kitchen extension with a flat roof. This can be broken down into elements and work content as follows:

Element	Work done by contractor	Work capable of being done by the average enthusiast
1. Foundations	Brickwork, concrete	Excavation
2. Roof	Felt	Joists, decking, fascia board, rainwater installation, painting
3. Internal and external walls	Brickwork, blockwork	–
4. Windows and doors	Joinery, glazing	Painting
5. Finishes	Screeding and floor tiling, plasterboard and plastering	Wall tiling

Element	Work done by contractor	Work capable of being done by the average enthusiast
6. Fittings	–	Kitchen units and worktops
7. Plumbing	–	Copper pipework, waste, soil and overflow, sink top and taps
8. Electrical work	Wiring, outlets, connection to existing	–
9. Drainage	Pipelaying, modifications to existing	Excavation and backfilling
10. External works	–	New paving

As you can see, as an average do-it-yourselfer, you could be capable of carrying out a large portion of the work involved. You must therefore decide which parts, if any, you will do yourself and which you will pay a contractor to do. There are several factors which must be considered here.

Time available

Generally speaking the do-it-yourself enthusiast will take longer to carry out the same work than a professional. You must therefore weigh the money you can save against the disadvantage of having your house disrupted for a longer period. This becomes especially relevant if there are young children to be considered or if the house is likely to be open to the wind and rain, especially in winter.

Programme of the work

The programming of the work is very important particularly if the work is substantial. You must avoid disrupting the contractor otherwise he may want to be paid extra money. For example, if you carry out the excavation as shown in the previous work plan you must ensure that the work is complete before the contractor arrives on site to carry out the concrete and brickwork. This applies to any aspect of the job which you decide to carry out yourself. You must consider not only whether you are capable of doing the work, but whether you can finish it within a set period of time. Don't forget that your good intentions can be upset by bad weather, illness, work or family problems.

Specialist work

Certain types of work such as electrical installations are better left to the experts unless you are absolutely assured of your own capabilities. Whilst the actual work involved in putting in a spur on a ring main is relatively simple, there are stringent regulations and safety aspects to be considered which you may not be aware of. It may seem a straightforward task to lay a 50 mm cement and sand floor screed, but it is extremely difficult to make the screed level and smooth enough to receive floor tiles. This type of work should therefore generally be left to the expert.

Cost

To the average person, cost will probably be the most important factor in deciding whether to do part of the work yourself, but you must be careful. It is easy to make a decision that could turn out to be a false economy. You must be absolutely sure of your ability to carry out the work properly first time round because it will prove far more costly to have the work put right if it is done incorrectly.

Think about the cost of your own time. If you are self employed or have a job which involves overtime, you may be financially better off working at your own job and having the construction work done for you. The value which you place on leisure time is also a consideration; do-it-yourself is a time consuming activity and you may often find that once a task has begun there is little spare time for anything else and the effect of this on your spouse and family should be considered very carefully. It can be seen that it may be wise not to make up your mind on the basis of money alone.

So remember:

1. Employ a contractor when the time available for any job is limited.
2. Only carry out parts of the work yourself if you are sure you will not interfere with the contractor's own programme.
3. Always use a contractor for specialist work unless you are absolutely sure you are capable of doing the work yourself.

Choosing a contractor

Deciding which contractor or contractors to use can be extremely difficult. When you are about to spend a large amount of money you have to be confident that it is going to be spent wisely. Everyone has heard horror stories about jobs that went wrong because the builder was a 'cowboy'. What can be done to prevent this happening to you? There are several important points to bear in mind.

1. Always be wary of people knocking on the door and trying to sell you something, whether it is double glazing or roof repairs. Do not be tempted by discounts offered for ordering the work there and then. You can rest assured that even if the salesman has to come back you will still get the discount if you give him the work.

2. Try and find a contractor by recommendation. Ask your friends and neighbours and then go and see examples of his work if at all possible.

3. If you decide to use your local Yellow Pages, try and pick a contractor who is affiliated to a national body, i.e. associations like the Federation of Master Builders, the Electrical Contractors' Association and the Institute of Plumbing. Some of them will provide guarantees of their members' work in return for a modest premium. In the case of the Federation of Master Builders, their warranty scheme would cost you only 1% of the value of the work (minimum fee £5). For this sum you receive protection against:

   (*a*) the cost of employing another contractor to complete the work if the first one stops trading;
   (*b*) a two year guarantee of materials and workmanship.

   Full details can be obtained from the Federation of Master Builders, Gordon Fisher House, 33 John Street, London WC1N 2BB (Telephone 01-242-7583).

4. Make sure that the contractor does all or most of the work himself and check which trades he sublets. Contractors who sublet all of their work are not really contractors but just middle men. Having lots of subcontractors doing the job in these circumstances is not likely to give you good value or good workmanship.

5. Only negotiate with a single contractor if you know him well or if he is highly recommended. Even in these circumstances it may be advisable to obtain alternative quotations to be absolutely sure that you are obtaining value for money. In all other instances approach two or three contractors for quotations. Any more than three may lead to unnecessary confusion when you compare their offers.

Obtaining estimates and quotations

Some contractors will tell you that there is a difference between an estimate and a quotation, although in law they are one and the same (see 'Making a simple contract' p.11). An estimate might be only an approximation of the cost of the work whereas a quotation is generally seen as an offer to do the work at the price quoted. However, many contractors see the two as the same, so it is always worth confirming with a contractor who says he will do the work for an 'estimate' that his price is firm and not subject to extra charges once the work is complete.

When obtaining quotations from more than one contractor, you must make sure that they are all based on an equal footing. It is no use telling one contractor that you want one type of floor tile and then telling another something entirely different. The best method of establishing this is to use the system of drawings and specification that the professionals use, but on a simplified basis.

Unless you have a knowledge of the building industry the chances are that the drawings for your kitchen extension will be done by a professional, either an architect, a building surveyor, or an advanced technician. As with obtaining quotations for the actual building of your extension, you should also shop around for these services.

For work valued at less than £20,000 architects would negotiate their fee (it is only subject to percentages above that figure) but it is likely that you will be charged between 10 and 12½% of the value of the work for a full service, i.e. obtaining planning permission, building regulations approval, preparing drawings, appointing a contractor and supervising the work. If you agree to pay on an hourly rate basis for professional sevices, make sure that you agree an overall ceiling figure and that you are advised at regular intervals how many hours have been spent on your work. The current rates are £15 to £20 per hour for an architect or surveyor and £9 to £11 for a technician.

Most of the actual technical specifications should appear on these drawings; plaster type and thicknesses, floor screed type and thickness and so on. All that would remain is for you to add your particular details; type of floor tile, type of kitchen fitting etc. Unlike the professionals who do this for a living, however, your knowledge of building workmanship will not be sufficient to enable you to specify everything necessary, and the actual workmanship of the job will generally be left up to the builder. As a general guide however, the following check list will be helpful:

Building element	Principal items to include in specification
Substructure	Concrete strength; type of brickwork and mortar; type of damp proof membrane and damp proof course.
Upper floor	Size and spacing of joists. Type and thickness of flooring.
Roof	Size and spacing of joists and other timber members such as fascia boards, soffit boards, etc; type of insulating material; type and thickness of roof covering and number of coats for flat roofs; type of roof tile, underlay and battens for pitched roofs; type and sizes of gutters and downspouts; type and thickness of flashings.
Walls	Type of brickwork and mortar and method of bonding and pointing; type and strength of blockwork; type of wall ties.
Windows	Sizes of members if not a standard window; type of ironmongery; type of glass and method of fixing; type and number of coats of paint; type and size of lintol.
Doors	Size of frame and architraves; type and size of door; type of ironmongery; type of glass and method of fixing; type and number of coats of paint; type and size of lintol.
Finishes	Thickness of floor screed; type of floor finish; type of skirting and decoration; type of plaster and number and thickness of coats; type of wall tiling; type of wall decoration; thickness of ceiling plasterboard; type and thickness of ceiling plaster; ceiling decoration.
Fittings	Details of cupboards, shelving and associated decoration.
Sanitary fittings	Type of sanitary fittings and colour; type of taps and traps.

Building element	Principal items to include in specification
Plumbing installation	Types and sizes of pipes for waste, soil and overflow and water installations; state whether to be exposed or concealed, and method of concealment.
Electrical installation	Type of fittings and outlets; state whether to be exposed or concealed and method of concealment.

There are many instances where you will not need to ask for a written quotation, for example; changing a tap washer. Where the work is so simple that there is very little chance of anything going wrong then a verbal quotation would be enough. However you should always ask for quotations on complete items of work, never on a time basis. The quotation for renewal of the tap washer should be an all in price for the actual removal and replacement of that washer not a price per hour for the actual time taken to do it. Beware of any quotations which have conditions attached to them: the price for doing that particular job will be a hundred pounds "*if*. . . etc, etc." Always try to have the 'if's' removed so that the contractor cannot come back when the job is done claiming extra money arguing that the 'if's' were not fulfilled. When obtaining quotations don't forget to clarify who will remove and replace all the existing carpets, fittings and furniture, and to spell out any restrictions you may want to make about the hours contractors will work and the parts of your house they may not use.

You should also discuss the question of the disposal of any surplus materials. If you want them taken away then tell the contractor. On the other hand, if you want your existing kitchen units carefully removed and left for use elsewhere or to be sold, then you must say so because this may influence the quotation price.

When the quotation arrives, make sure that it covers everything that you want. Written quotations should be detailed enough to enable you to check that you are receiving what you are paying for; they should also make it possible to value any extras or variations that may occur. However you should not expect every single nut and bolt to appear on the quotation, only the principal items.

Quotations may take several different forms because each contractor will have his own particular method of pricing work. At the very least it should list the principal materials priced separately and show the labour, plant and VAT. It should also be clear and unambiguous and contain all the points raised in any discussions. You will probably find it helpful to take notes of telephone calls and discussions with the contractor. Details of how long the job will take and when it will start should also be included in the quotation, together with the course of action to be taken if the work takes any longer (see 'Making a simple contract' p.11). The other two main items which should be included are details of payments and the valuing of variations and extras, both of which are discussed separately later in this chapter.

Finally, it is most important that you read all of the quotation. Many contractors have standard conditions of sale on the back of quotations or fastened to them. You must study them carefully. If there is anything you are not happy about, you should bring it to the contractor's attention and have it changed or taken out. Under no circumstance accept items you are not satisfied with. Once you are happy with the quotation the only thing which needs to be done is to accept it. A verbal acceptance is sufficient and would constitute a binding agreement but it is always preferable to have the acceptance made in writing. Having signed your acceptance ask for a copy of the quotation and keep it somewhere safe.

Payment

Payment can be the cause of much dispute between contractor and client but difficulties can be avoided by agreeing the method of payment at the start and including it in the written quotation.

There are several ways of making payments to the contractor depending upon the individual circumstances of the job.

Payment before the work commences

This is not recommended except where the amount involved is relatively small, the time to do the job is short, and the contractor involved is of unquestionable character and reputation. In any event there is no point in making payment in advance unless there is some benefit to be gained by doing so, e.g. by obtaining a reduction of the quotation price.

Payment after the work is complete

This is obviously the most desirable method for the householder but the contractor would probably resist this arrangement unless the job was of low value and could be done quickly. It is not suitable for high value jobs which may take several weeks or months to complete, particularly for small contractors who may experience cash flow problems.

Payment on a stage basis

There are two main methods of doing this. The first is to pay on percentages of the total value at agreed intervals. If the job was scheduled to take three months, one third of the price might be paid each month. This method is not recommended because it does not take progress into account and could result in the payments being in advance of the value of the work completed which would reduce the contractor's motivation to finish the job. The second method is to pay agreed amounts at various completed stages of the work. In the example of a house extension these stages could be agreed as:

(*a*) foundations and ground floor slab;
(*b*) external walls and roof;
(*c*) completion.

Payment for materials as they are supplied

Here you pay the cost of the materials as they are delivered, with the balance paid when the work is complete. To do this properly you should ask the contractor for copies of his material invoices, although they may not always be available if he is operating on a credit system with his suppliers. If the contractor is unable to provide invoices then it may be necessary to agree the value of the materials in advance.

Variations and extras

It is true to say that unforeseen extras to the original work are probably the largest single cause of disputes, but the problem can be avoided in most cases. Variations, or 'extras' as they are commonly known, may arise for all sorts of reasons, and who pays for them will depend upon the reasons for the extra occurring. Variations can be categorised under three headings.

1. Those which the contractor is instructed to make – if you ask for a cast iron bath complete with solid gold taps instead of the plastic type which you originally requested, then you should expect to pay the difference in price.

2. Items which the contractor should have included in the original quotation – if you had always wanted a cast iron bath with gold

fittings and the drawings or specification said so, then it is obviously the contractor's mistake if he only priced for a plastic type and he should bear the cost. Variations or extras of this type can often be avoided by insisting on detailed quotations and examining them carefully.

3. Changes which are due to the contractor having to carry out work different from that foreseen at the time the work was quoted for – in this case the liability for the additional cost may not be so clear cut. For instance, the contractor may have thought he could run his plumbing pipework in the floor space but subsequently found that the floor was solid. Who then would be liable for the extra cost of cutting channels? Remember that if your house has fitted carpets throughout this may have prevented him from making a detailed examination at the quotation stage. In this example it is considered that the responsibility lies with the contractor and he should bear the additional cost. If, however, rotten floorboards are discovered upon removing the bath, it is only fair that you should pay extra for their renewal because it would have been unreasonable for the contractor to have assumed the defect and included the cost in his quotation. There are times when the problem is not as black and white as these examples and if there is a genuine doubt over liability, then a fair cost-sharing arrangement should be considered.

The valuation of variations and extras can also cause much disagreement but with a little forethought, arguments can be kept to a minimum. The first step in avoiding disputes is to ensure the original quotation is as detailed as reasonably possible. A quotation which simply says 'Kitchen extension as designed and detailed – £14,000' is of little use when it comes to the valuation of extras. A detailed quotation can form the basis for valuing extras, particularly if the additional work is the same or of a similar character to an item which appears separately in the quotation.

A detailed quotation can also prevent arguments about what was included in the original price if variations occur. Even then it may not be possible to relate the cost of extra work to an item in the original quotation so the work must be valued in another manner. The best method is to ask for a firm quotation for the extra work in advance. In this way you will know the cost beforehand and be able to decide whether you can afford to have the additional work carried out. You should not under any circumstances request additional work without knowing the cost nor should you agree to additional work being done on a 'time to do it' (sometimes called 'time and lime'!) basis. Remember also that leaving out work is also a variation and the same rules apply. All variations should be recorded in writing and signed by both you and the contractor. This will enable you to keep a record of your overall expenditure and will also save time when the final bill is presented.

From your point of view it is obviously better to leave the payment for extras until the end of the job. However, the contractor may request that they are paid for as and when they are complete; this is perfectly reasonable. As with any transaction however, you should ask for proof of payment and if you have followed the advice on agreeing and recording any variations then the contractor simply stamps or writes 'paid' on the agreement sheet together with his signature.

Making a simple contract

The law of contract has evolved from the many cases which have passed through the English court system. Contract law is a varied and complex subject and outside the scope of this book. But when you employ a contractor to do your work, you are creating a contract and it is important that you understand the basic rules that apply.

A simple contract is made when an offer is made by one person and accepted by another. The contract is only enforceable in law however, when there is also consideration involved. Consideration is the reward or gain that the person making the offer receives in return for fulfilling the terms of the offer. In the case of a kitchen extension, the offer would be made by the contractor to construct the extension, the acceptance would be made by you saying 'yes go ahead' and the consideration would be the amount of money to be paid to the contractor in return for completing the job. It is not strictly necessary for the offer and acceptance to be written down. But if it is not, and the job goes wrong and ends up in the courts, there would be obvious problems over the establishment of proof. These problems would not arise if the parties record their intentions in writing. It should be noted that the consideration does not have to be a sum, it can just as easily be an intention. For instance it is no defence to say that there was no enforceable contract because you had not agreed to a price if it could be reasonably inferred that you had accepted the offer with the 'intention' to pay. Nor is it necessary for a contractor to say 'I *offer* to do the work for £1,000' he could just as easily say 'My estimate to do the work is £1,000'. This would constitute a binding offer.

The offer may be withdrawn at any time by the contractor before acceptance but once the acceptance has been communicated to the contractor it cannot be revoked or withdrawn. Note that the actual posting of an acceptance letter constitutes acceptance, but a posted withdrawal of an offer is not effective until received.

Another important point to note in contract law is that an offer is made invalid if a counter offer is made. For example the contractor offers to build you a kitchen extension for £14,000 but you think this is too expensive and make a counter offer of £12,500 which the contractor rejects. After shopping around you find that the cheapest you can have the job done for is £15,500 and go back to the original contractor and agree to accept his original asking price. Even if the contractor has not formally withdrawn his original offer he is not bound now to stand by it, because by making the counter offer you have invalidated it. An offer is also invalid if not accepted within a reasonable time. There are no rules defining how long is a 'reasonable' time.

Assuming that a valid contract exists between yourself and the contractor, the question may arise of how much compensation, if any, you are entitled to if the contractor does not carry out his obligations, and so breaks the contract.

Damages are the law's method of compensating the injured party for injury, damage or loss. Thus, if you have suffered damage, injury or loss, and you can prove that it was incurred as a direct result of the broken contract, then you would be entitled to damages. Damages represent compensation: they are only awarded to recompense for the actual loss suffered and are not used in order to penalise or punish the contract breaker. The value of damages may be difficult to ascertain. For example, the contractor may take twice as long to complete your kitchen extension as he originally contracted to do. You may be entitled to damages even though you have not lost any money, because damages may be paid for physical inconvenience. They may also be awarded for the mental anguish you have suffered, although this is more difficult to prove.

If your contractor leaves the job incomplete or badly done, you may be entitled to the cost of having the work rectified or completed. You are, by the way, more likely to succeed in your case if you have first tried to have the work put right by the original contractor.

If you should find yourself in the unfortunate position of having to claim against a contractor, how do you go about it? The first course of action is to try to get the contractor to put the job right himself, if necessary by threatening him with legal action. Make your requests in writing and see that they are delivered via a recorded delivery system. Keep copies of all correspondence. Make notes of the times, dates and contents of any telephone conversations. If there is no reply or your requests are rejected, then your only remedy is through the court. Before you decide to sue however, you should make sure that not only do you have a good case, but that if you win, the contractor has the means to pay the amount of the award.

Your claim will normally be heard in the County Court and the procedure in taking out a court action is well defined. A good reference is the form EX50 'Small Claims in the County Court' which can be obtained from the County Court, a Law Centre or a Citizens Advice Bureau. This outlines the procedure for bringing a small claim to court without going to the expense of hiring a solicitor. You should also bear in mind that you may also be entitled to legal aid depending upon your financial status; you should ask your local Legal Aid Office or Citizens Advice Bureau. If the claim warrants the use of a solicitor then try and find one who is used to dealing with your type of case. Remember again to shop around because charges vary. It is advisable to ask the solicitor if he does an initial consultation at a special fee or even free, which would then give you some idea of the likely success of your claim.

Programming

If you are an enthusiastic do-it-yourselfer with a reasonable level of skill, you will probably want to carry out part of the work on your kitchen extension yourself. There are two choices:

(*a*) let the other work to a contractor;

or

(*b*) let the other work to individual tradesmen.

If the extension has to be completed within a fixed period of time then careful co-ordination and planning of the work is required. This is most easily done by preparing a simple bar chart (see chart below). This shows the anticipated programme of the kitchen extension in a form which is easy to follow. The main items of work are on the vertical scale with the horizontal scale representing time. As can be seen certain work items cannot start before others have been completed, e.g. the roof cannot commence until the external walls are built. The chart shows how your work affects that to be done by the contractor and this should help to monitor progress.

If you are going to let the balance of the work to tradesmen then care has to be exercised in making sure the tradesmen arrive at the right time to carry out their particular work. This must be given careful thought. But there are financial benefits in doing the work this way because you are cutting out the profit of the main builder.

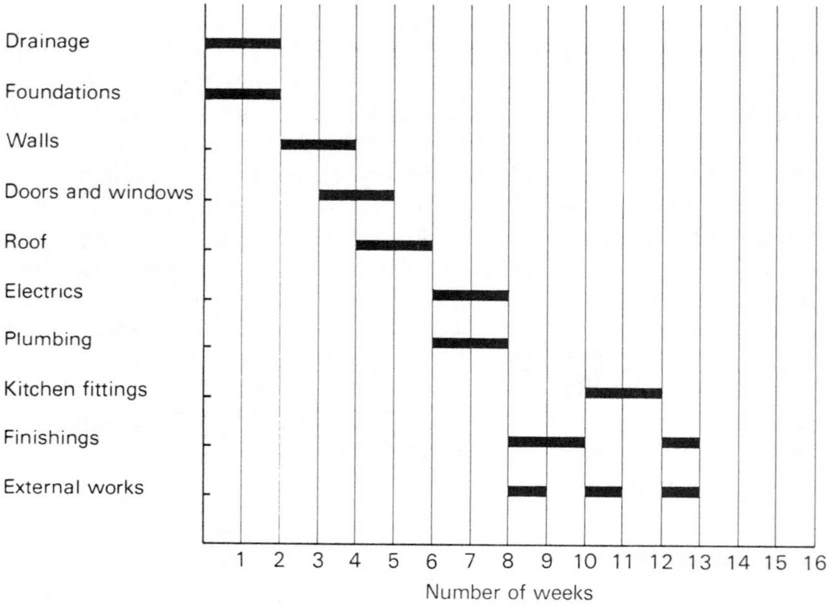

Design and build by a contractor

Quite often you may find it easier and cheaper to use a contractor for a complete service rather than having separate drawings done, obtaining planning and building regulation approval and then finding a contractor to do the work. This system, whereby the contractor produces the drawings, obtains the necessary approvals and does the physical work on site is commonly known as 'design and build' and it can have several advantages. You will only be dealing with one person so there is less likelihood of misunderstandings. If you choose a contractor who is used to doing this sort of scheme you will benefit by his knowledge of the most economic method of carrying out your particular job. He will also be able to advise you on the best choice of materials because he may have special rates of discount with certain suppliers that he can then pass on to you. However it is not guaranteed to be cheaper doing it this way (apart from the possible savings listed). You will still have to pay for the design and drawings, building regulations and planning fees although these will not necessarily be shown separately on the quotation. There are also potential disadvantages. For the very same reasons that a contractor may be able to obtain special discount for certain materials, he may also try and force these upon you, when you may not really want them. He may also try to use up stocks of existing materials lying around his yard. You must therefore be strong minded about what you want without being unreasonable. A big advantage of this system is that an experienced contractor will be able to guide you on what your improvements are going to cost as you develop your thoughts. But it is safe to say that you are probably more at risk from the unscrupulous contractor because you become totally reliant on him without anyone else to look after your interests. You must be particularly careful in your choice of contractor when adopting this method.

The same can also be said of standard or prefabricated systems such as precast concrete garages or house extensions. Here again personal recommendation is desirable if not essential. You should not overlook the small local specialist in preference to the larger national people. The larger companies rely heavily upon advertising on a national scale which can be very expensive and must be paid for by the customer. On the other hand the products of the national company which has been trading for some years are usually tried and tested and of course the major advantage lies in the speed of erection compared to traditional methods of construction.

There is no easy method of finding out which contractor is giving you the best value for money with design and build because it is difficult to compare quotations. You will have to rely upon your instinct to some extent but in any case you should always establish whether the contractor will charge you for the cost of design if you do not proceed with the actual construction and if so, how much it will be. If you consider this to be excessive, then you may be able to negotiate a reduction, or if that fails approach someone else.

DIY
BRICKLAYING

2 Doing it yourself

Measuring

Before tackling any DIY task it will be necessary to order materials and this will probably involve you in 'measuring up'. A retractable steel measure is the most convenient tool to use and the following simple rules should enable you to calculate the area of most shapes.

Rectangle For the area, multiply the length by the width. Remember that if the shape you are measuring is irregular, it is usually quicker to calculate the overall area and deduct the voids (see Fig. 1)

28 × 20	=		560
Deduct			
3 × 16	=	48	
5 × 8	=	40	
3 × 17	=	51	139
			421 sq ft

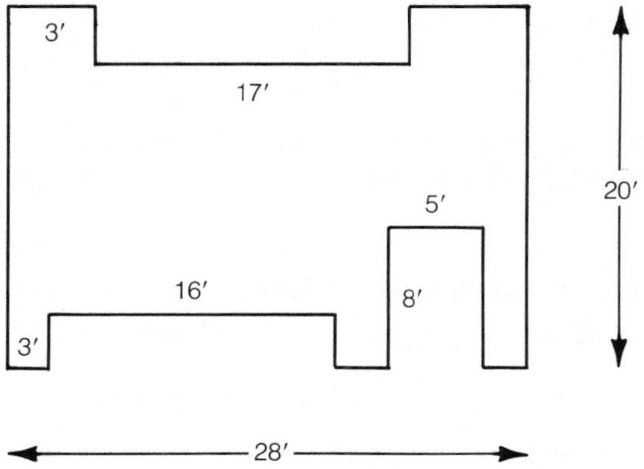

Fig. 1

If Fig. 1 represented the floor plan of a kitchen, you may also wish to measure the perimeter of the room for a cornice or skirting. This is done quite simply by adding the width and length and multiplying by two. There is no need to work your way round all the indentations.

$$(28 + 20) \times 2 = 96 \text{ ft}$$

If this calculation was needed for the total length of a skirting you should, of course, deduct any door openings and the like. The assessed perimeter of 96 ft could also be used as a basis for working out the wall area by multiplying it by the storey height (the height from floor to ceiling). If it was 7′6″, the wall area would be 96′ × 7′6″ = 720 sq ft divided by 9 = 80 sq yds (less openings).

Triangle The triangular area is half the base multiplied by the perpendicular height (see Fig. 2)

i.e. $\frac{1}{2} \times 6 \times 4 = 12$ sq ft

This rule applies to all shapes and sizes of triangles. There is no simple way of calculating the perimeter – you just add the lengths of the three sides together.

Fig. 2

There may be a need sometimes to calculate the area or volume of other shapes and the following tables may prove helpful.

Circumference or perimeters of planes

Circle	3.1416 × diameter
Ellipse	3.1416 × ½(major axis + minor axis)
Sector	$\frac{\text{Radius} \times \text{degrees in arc}}{57.3}$

Surface areas of planes and solids

Circle	Pi (3.1416) × radius^2 or 0.7854 × diameter
Cone	½ Circumference × slant height + area of base
Frustum of cone	Pi (3.1416) × slant height × (radius at top + radius at base) + area of top and base
Cylinder	(Circumference × length) + area of two ends
Ellipse (approx.)	Product of axes × 0.7854
Parallelo-gram	Base × height
Pyramid	½ (base perimeter × slant height) + area of base
Sector of circle	$\frac{3.1416 \times \text{degrees in arc} \times \text{radius}^2}{360}$
Sphere	Diameter^2 × 3.1416

Volumes

Cone	Area of base × ½ perpendicular height
Cylinder	3.1416 × radius^2 × height
Pyramid	Area of base × ¼ perpendicular height

Ordering materials

The demand for DIY materials has increased enormously in recent years and most areas have a choice of retail units. Probably the most significant change has been the introduction of the national DIY superstore. These stores can supply most DIY materials and because they buy in large quantities, they are usually very competitive with builder's merchants. Although some of these outlets have a delivery service, they are usually cash and carry but you would still need to go to a merchant for items like bricks and cement unless you were buying very small quantities.

The ordering of materials is not always straightforward. For instance take a cubic yard of concrete. You cannot go out and order a cubic yard of concrete (unless it is ready mix). You must have knowledge of the weight of the cement, sand and aggregate and you must remember the wastage factor. You may find that using only part of a bag of cement is more expensive than buying a premixed bag of concrete of the right quantity. Some thought must go into ordering materials to prevent waste, and the following information will assist you.

Please note that although most of the information in Chapters 4 and 6 is given in both imperial and metric, some of the following materials are only stated in metric terms because that is how they are sold.

Excavation work

Material bulks when dug out, i.e. it occupies a greater volume after it has been excavated. It would be wrong to order a ten cubic yards skip for ten cubic yards of excavation because the skip would be too small to receive the bulked material. The following are average percentage bulking increases for various types of ground:

Sand/gravel	10-15%
Ordinary clay, etc.	20-30%
Hard materials, rock, etc.	40-50%

Concrete work – mixed by hand

The two most common concrete mixes are 1:3:6 and 1:2:4. Usually you would use 1:3:6 in foundations and 1:2:4 in walls, paths and the like. These are the proportions by volume of the cement:sand:aggregate respectively. In other words there is one part cement, three parts of sand and six parts of aggregate or gravel in a 1:3:6 mix. But these materials are usually sold by weight and you must know what the proportions are by dry weight for each cubic metre of concrete mixed.

	1 cubic yard		1 cubic metre	
	1:2:4	1:3:6	1:2:4	1:3:6
Cement	400 lb	290 lb	240 kg	170 kg
Sand	900 lb	950 lb	520 kg	550 kg
Aggregate	1600 lb	1700 lb	950 kg	1000 kg

If you were laying a foundation for a garden wall you should first calculate the volume of the concrete. Say it was 30 feet long × 1 foot wide × 6 inches deep (approximately 9 metres × 300 mm wide × 150 mm deep) which produces a volume of 15 cubic feet, i.e. 15/27 or 0.55 cubic yards (0.41 cubic metres).

If the foundation was to be laid in 1:3:6 mix you would need to order the following quantities of materials including the 5% allowance for waste.

0.55 cubic yards		0.41 cubic metres	
Cement			
290 + 5% × 0.55	= 170 lb	170 + 5% × 0.41	= 73 kg
Sand			
950 + 5% × 0.55	= 550 lb	550 + 5% × 0.41	= 237 kg
Aggregate			
1700 + 5% × 0.55	= 980 lb	1000 + 5% × 0.41	= 430 kg

It is unlikely that you will be able to buy the exact quantities you require but you should be able to cut down on waste by being aware of what you actually need.

Ready mixed concrete

For large jobs it is probably easier to order the concrete ready mixed. Most ready mixed wagons carry 4, 5 or 6 cubic metres of concrete and will deliver part loads but you will have to pay above the full load unit price. Look in your Yellow Pages and you will probably find a firm who specialise in delivering small quantities.

One tip worth remembering is to have somewhere in your garden ready to receive any concrete left over from the job you are carrying out. A little forethought can provide a path extension or a base for a future coal bunker instead of an unsightly heap of unwanted concrete.

Brickwork

The most common size of bricks is approximately 9″ × 4½″ × 3″ (215 × 102.5 × 65 mm) and the following information is based on the use of bricks of this size:

Number of bricks per square metre of wall per half brick thickness	= 59

The number of facing bricks per square metre of one brick thick wall depends upon the bond used.The following table gives the number of facing bricks in walls faced one side only.

Stretcher bond	59
Header bond	118
English bond	90
Flemish bond	80
English garden wall bond	75
Flemish garden wall bond	68

Add to the above for wastage – 5%.

Mortar

Mortar below ground level is usually a 1:3 cement:sand mix and above ground a cement:lime:sand mortar (known as gauged mortar) either 1:1:6 or 1:2:9. Here are the approximate dry weights of materials for each of the above mixes per cubic metre of mixed material:

	Cement mortar (1:3)	Gauged mortar (1:1:6)	Gauged mortar (1:2:9)
Cement	440 kg	230 kg	160 kg
Lime	–	120 kg	160 kg
Sand	1820 kg	1920 kg	1980 kg

Add to the above for wastage – 7½%.

The average quantity of mortar per square metre half brick wall is 0.03 cu m. Wall ties should be used at the rate of three per square metre of cavity.

Woodwork

When buying timber, you should always try and buy lengths which are slightly longer than those you require in order to reduce wastage.

Add for wastage when ordering – 7½%.

Don't forget, these prices may need adjustment depending on where you live.
Regional adjustments are provided on the inside cover, and further explanation is given in the Preface.

Floor and wall tiles

Use this table to work out how many tiles you need:

Tile size (mm)	Number of tiles per square metre
100 × 100	100
150 × 75	89
150 × 150	44
200 × 100	33
200 × 200	25
225 × 225	20
250 × 62	65
250 × 125	32
250 × 250	16
300 × 150	22
300 × 300	11
450 × 450	5
600 × 600	3
600 × 450	4

The wastage on tiles depends upon several factors: size and shape of room, pattern, size of tile, type of material and hardness.

As an average add 7½% to the above figure for waste.

See if you can obtain refunds if you return unopened packs. If you have to purchase further packs ask whether any discount you may have been given on purchase will still apply.

Painting

The covering capacity of paints varies enormously depending upon the nature of the surface, type of paint, skill of the painter and the following figures should only be taken as a guide. Manufacturers often indicate their own coverage capacities on the can and these may be more accurate than the following figures which are issued by the Paint and Painting Industries' Liaison Committee. The figures quoted are practical figures for brush application, achieved in scale painting work and take into account losses and wastage. They are not optimum figures based upon ideal conditions of surface, nor minimum figures reflecting the reverse of these conditions. The figures are quoted in square metres per litre, except for cement based paint which are in square metres per kilogram (see below):

The texture of roughcast and pebbledash can vary markedly and you could find significant variations in the coverage of paints applied to these surfaces. The figures given are typical but under some conditions much lower coverages could be obtained. In many instances the coverages achieved will be affected by the suction and texture of the backing.

	A	B	C	D	E	F	G	H
Water thinned primer/undercoat								
as primer	13-15	–	–	–	–	10-14	–	–
as undercoat	–	–	–	–	–	12-15	12-15	–
Plaster primer	9-11	8-12	7-9	5-7	2-4	–	–	–
Alkali resistant primer	7-11	6-8	6-8	4-6	2-4	–	–	–
External wall primer sealer	6-8	6-7	5-7	4-6	2-4	–	–	–
Undercoat	11-14	7-9	6-8	6-8	3-4	10-12	11-14	–
Gloss finish	11-14	8-10	7-9	6-8	–	10-12	11-14	11-14
Emulsion paint								
standard	12-15	8-12	8-12	6-10	2-4	10-12	12-15	12-15
contract	10-12	7-11	7-10	5-9	2-4	10-12	10-12	10-12
Heavy texture coating	2-4	2-4	2-4	2-4	2-4	2-4	2-4	2-4
Masonry paint	5-7	4-6	4-6	3-5	2-4	–	6-8	6-8
Cement based paint (per kilo)	–	4-6	3-6	3-6	2-3	–	–	–
Wood primer (oil based)	–	–	–	–	–	8-11	–	–

Key

A – Finishing plaster
B – Wood floated rendering
C – Fair faced brickwork
D – Blockwork
E – Rough cast/pebbledash
F – Woodwork
G – Smooth primed surfaces
H – Smooth undercoated surfaces

Paper hanging

The amount of wallpaper needed to decorate a room will depend on the length of the pattern repeat, the number of doors and windows and the room height. The following table gives the approximate number of rolls required for various size rooms and heights.

Height of papered wall	Total perimeter of room				
	8. 5 m	11 m	13.5 m	16 m	18 m
2.10-2.25 m	4	5	6	7	8
2.25-2.40 m	4	5	6	7	8
2.40-2.55 m	4	5	6	7	8
2.55-2.70 m	4	5	7	8	9
2.70-2.85 m	4	6	7	8	9
2.85-3.00 m	5	6	7	9	10
3.00-3.15 m	5	6	8	9	10
	20.5 m	23 m	25.5 m	28 m	30.5 m
2.10-2.25 m	9	9	10	11	12
2.25-2.40 m	9	10	11	12	13
2.40-2.55 m	9	10	12	13	14
2.55-2.70 m	10	11	12	13	15
2.70-2.85 m	10	12	13	14	15
2.85-3.00 m	11	12	14	15	16
3.00-3.15 m	12	13	14	16	17

Building regulations

When carrying out home improvements, planning permission and building regulations must be considered. Building regulations deal with the health and safety of people and also with energy conservation.

The latest edition of the Building Regulations was published in 1985 by Her Majesty's Stationery Office (HMSO) and there are copies in most libraries. Building Regulations approval must be obtained whenever a new building or an extension is proposed. However, there are instances when approval is not required. These include:

(*a*) if the new building is erected for certain types of specialised use, such as temporary site huts and small detached buildings not exceeding thirty square metres, with no sleeping accommodation;

(*b*) when a greenhouse, conservatory, porch, covered way or covered yard with a total floor area not exceeding thirty square metres, is added to an existing building.

You must get approval if the existing building fabric would be materially altered by the proposed work, i.e. where it affects the structure, means of escape, or if the speed at which flame can spread both internally and externally necessitates the insertion of insulating materials in a cavity or underpinning.

If you propose to make certain alterations to building services, approval may also be required. These include the provision, extension or alteration of sanitary equipment, drainage, vented hot water systems, fixed heating appliances in which fuel is burnt; but not in small buildings not exceeding thirty square metres as previously defined.

Approval may also be required if you propose a change in the use of an existing building or if the building is to be converted to living accommodation or for public use where previously it was not.

There are two ways you can ensure that your improvements comply with the Building Regulations. The first method is to get forms from your local building control officer which will explain precisely what is required. The second method is to appoint a private approved inspector to oversee the work. These persons must be independent and the building being improved and the appointment is subject to the Building (Approved Inspectors) Regulations 1985.

The plans, drawings and other particulars submitted for approval must be detailed enough for the local authority or approved inspector to establish that the work complies with the Building Regulations. Amendments or modifications may be made or requested if the Regulations are being broken and these must be complied with. The amount and level of information which you must submit varies according to the type of work involved and you should read the Regulations for guidance.

You must pay fees in connection with applications for Building Regulations approval. These fees are fixed by the Building (Prescribed Fees, etc.) Regulations 1985. The fees charged cover the inspection of plans and other particulars and the inspection of the work in progress. There are several scales of fees depending upon the nature of the work involved. As an illustration the following are the current fees for work to small garages, carports and certain alterations and extensions.

Type of work	Plan fee	Inspection fee
1. An extension or alteration consisting of the provision of one or more rooms in roof space including means of access	£22 + VAT	£66 + VAT
2. Any extension (not falling within paragraph 1 above) which does not have a total floor area exceeding 20 square metres	£11 + VAT	£33 + VAT
3. Any extension (not falling within paragraph 1 above) which has a floor area of between 20 square metres and 40 square metres	£22 + VAT	£66 + VAT

The plan fee is payable when you hand in the plans and you will have to pay the inspection fee after the inspection has been made.

Details of fees for other types of work should be obtained from your local authority.

Planning permission

You may also have to obtain planning permission for your home improvement but it depends upon the nature of the work you intend carrying out. All developments are controlled by planning laws in order to protect the interest of the public in development and use of land. Planning approvals are quite different from Building Regulations approvals and you may need both.

You should check with your local planning authority whether you need planning permission for the work you intend to do. However, you will need planning permission in the cases listed below.

1. If the work will obstruct the view of vehicular traffic using a highway thereby causing danger.

2. If the work will involve a new access to a trunk or classified road, or the widening of an existing one.

3. If the original planning approval for your house has restrictions on the types of work which can be done. These rules do not necessarily mean that you cannot do such work, only that you must apply for planning permission.

4. If you live in a listed building, National Park, Area of Outstanding Natural Beauty or Conservation Area, which was designated before 1 April 1981, then the rules governing your planning application may be more stringent and permission will often have to be obtained for work which would not otherwise require it. The local planning authority has the right to impose stricter controls. These are generally only in conservation areas or places where the authority wish to preserve the appearance or character. This is done by what is called an 'Article 4 direction' and the planning authority is obliged to inform you if an Article 4 direction affects your property. If in doubt you should check with your local authority.

5. If the work involves building over a sewer or drain you will have to obtain the consent of the local council under the 1936 Public Health Act.

6. Construction of an access, path or driveway to the road unless the access is to an unclassified road and necessary because of the construction of an extension, porch or hardstanding where planning permission is not required (see later). If the access path or driveway crosses a verge or path in order to meet the road however, the permission of the highway authority must always be given.

7. If you intend to use part of your house as an office to run a business or to let as bedsitters.

8. If you intend to use your house or associated buildings to store goods in connection with your business or sell goods from your house.

9. Conversion of your house or any part of it into flats.

10. Additions of a separate building attached to your house or otherwise to be used as an individual dwelling.

If your property is leasehold or if you are a tenant, then your lease or tenancy agreement may not allow you to carry out certain work even if you have planning permission so before you apply for permission under these circumstances, always check your agreement.

There may be a restrictive covenant which affects your property even if you own the property and if it is freehold. Look closely at your deeds to ensure that no restrictive covenants apply. If they do, check with your planning authority to see if there is any way round them and if necessary seek legal advice.

The following list shows the type of work where you do not need planning permission but if you are in any doubt, you should talk to your local planning officer.

1. General redecoration, maintenance or improvement work which does not increase the size of your property. Replacement windows providing they do not project beyond the most forward part of any wall of the original house. Changing the outside appearance of your property (pebbledashing, stone facing, etc.)

2. Internal alterations to the property providing that the internal use of the property is not changed.

3. House extensions provided that:

   (*a*) the volume of the house does not increase by 50 cubic metres, or one tenth of the volume of the original house up to a maximum of 115 cubic metres, whichever is the greater, for a terraced house, or house in a National Park, Area of Outstanding Natural Beauty or Conservation Area designated as such before 1 April 1981. For all other houses the limit is the greater size of 70 cubic metres or 15 per cent of the original house volume up to a maximum of 115 cubic metres;
   (*b*) extension is no higher than the original roof;
   (*c*) no part of the extension projects beyond the most forward part of any wall of the original house which faces a highway;
   (*d*) no part of the extension which is within two metres of the boundary is over four metres high (this does not apply to alterations and extensions to the original roof);
   (*e*) the extension does not cover more than half of the original garden area;
   (*f*) the extension is not intended as a separate or independent dwelling;

   (Note that the original volume is the external volume of the house as originally built or as it stood on 1 July 1984 if built before then).

4. Conservatories providing they are attached to the house and meet the conditions for house extensions.

5. Small buildings not attached to the house such as greenhouses, sheds, providing:

   (*a*) that the building is for the use of the occupants of the house;
   (*b*) the building does not project beyond the most forward part of any wall of the original house which faces a highway;
   (*c*) the height of the building does not exceed three metres (four metres if the roof is ridged).

6. Garages within five metres of the house or garages in National Parks, Areas of outstanding Natural Beauty or Conservation Areas designated before 1 April 1981, providing they meet the criteria for house extensions. Garages over five metres from the house are treated in the same way as small buildings.

7. Loft conversions providing the overall volume of the house does not increase otherwise it is classed as an extension.

8. Porches providing the floor area does not exceed 2 square metres, the height does not exceed 3 metres and it is over 2 metres from any boundary between the garden and road or footpath.

9. Television aerials providing they are the normal type attached to the house and used for domestic purposes.

10. Fences providing they do not exceed one metre in height where they run along a boundary which adjoins a vehicular highway or where they do not exceed two metres in height for other locations.

11. Hardstandings for private cars providing they are in your garden.

12. Cutting down trees unless they are covered by a Tree Preservation order or are in a Conservation Area.

13. Demolition of part of your house or building in the garden unless the building is listed or in a conservation area.

You must of course pay for making a planning application and the application fee at September 1988 for an alteration/extension varies from £33 for a basic extension up to £66 maximum and is dependent upon the size of the extension in relation to the existing property. If you decide to change the use or convert to flats, then different fees are chargeable and you should consult your local planning officer. There are exceptions however and these are:

(*a*) if the work is for the benefit of a disabled person;
(*b*) where circumstances dictate that the work required a planning application when under normal circumstances it would not – because of an Article 4 direction;
(*c*) if the application is a variant of a previously unsuccessful application and is made within twelve months of the unsuccessful application, or where an application which has been successful is withdrawn. Only one exemption is allowed for any particular work on your property.

In order to make a planning application you must contact your local planning authority who will send you the relevant forms for completion. In most cases it is better to submit a full and formal application at the beginning. This would mean supplying copies of a plan of the site and sufficient plans, drawings and information to enable the work to be identified clearly and without ambiguity. Your application will be put on the planning register which is open to examination by anyone. Depending on the authority, it may be advertised in the local press, and you may be required to display a notice outside your property or notify your immediate neighbours. Objections to your application may be lodged with the planning authority but no one can insist on a refusal of your application. That decision lies solely with the authority.

Should the authority reject your application they must give you the reasons for doing so. It may be that a re-submission will be successful if you can satisfy their objections by making suitable amendments to the work in order to accommodate them. However if you feel that their decision is unjust or that conditions imposed on an otherwise successful application are too onerous then you have the right to appeal. Appeals are heard by the Secretary of State for the Environment (or the Secretary of State for Scotland or Wales.) If you wish to appeal you must do so within six months of the original decision. However it is worth noting that more appeals fail than are successful although there is no fee charged for making an appeal.

Home Improvements – are they worth it?

With certain exceptions, you are wasting your money improving your home if you intend moving within a couple of years! There are many reasons for this which are explained later but the general rule is that you should only carry out the kind of improvements listed in this book if you intend to enjoy the amenity yourself. There is a wealth of evidence to show that the cost of constructing extensions, swimming pools, second bathrooms, through lounges and porches will not be recovered in the subsequent sale of the house.

The exceptions are central heating, garages and to a lesser extent double glazing and if you are lucky you may recover up to 75% of their construction costs. Another exception lies in the prospective purchaser himself. You may be lucky enough to find a buyer with exactly the same taste and family and social needs as you but it is extremely unlikely.

A further exception exists in periods of housing shortages when property value is increasing because of the demand. The cost of the improvements will be recovered but only because of the general lifting of house prices and not because of the intrinsic value of the improvement.

Most estate agents will tell you (although you could argue that they have a vested interest in promoting this view!) that if you have a need for an extra bedroom it is better to change house and move up the housing quality ladder, than build an extension. This theory is based upon the premise that it is more sensible to live in a £40,000 house surrounded by £60,000 value houses than in a £40,000 house (say £30,000 + £10,000 extension costs) in a £30,000 area. It follows on, of course, from this argument that you would be prudent to invest £10,000 in a house extension only if it will bring the value of the house up to that of your neighbours.

It is important to remember that all these comments are related to improvements. Carrying out maintenance such as re-wiring, pointing, damp-coursing, roof repairs and the like are part of any householder's duties and the selling price will drop in favour of the purchaser if they are neglected.

Another useful tip to remember when considering improving your house is that it is very important to maintain the balance of room uses. In other words, providing a second bathroom in a house with only three bedrooms is extravagant (unless of course, as stated earlier, you intend to enjoy the amenity yourself over a number of years). Similarly, constructing a fourth bedroom in a house with only one general purpose sitting room would also be unwise.

The following table shows the percentage of construction costs likely to be recovered if the property is sold within two years of the work being carried out.

Central heating	50-75	Sun lounge	10-30
Garage	50-75	Bedroom extension	0-20
Double glazing	40-50	Kitchen extension	0-20
Loft conversion	20-40	Porch	0-10
Basement conversion	20-40		

Safety

Whether or not you take out insurance you owe it to yourself, your family and anyone else on or near to the site to ensure that there are no unnecessary hazards around. Most accidents on construction sites are caused by slipping, tripping or falling, and from electrical shock. A few helpful 'do's and don'ts' are:

1. Plan the job in advance. Make sure you have all the tools and materials to do the job and that the tools are safe and efficient. Inspect all ladders and steps for defects and make sure they are of adequate length. Examine electric plugs, cables and sockets for correct type and that they are in good condition.
2. Clear the site of all unwanted furniture and equipment, make sure the family know of any 'no-go' areas. Wear overalls or similar clothing including a safety helmet and slip-resistant soles where appropriate. Secure ladders to avoid slipping. Check position of water pipes, electric cables etc.
3. While the work is in progress:
   - Don't leave tools and materials around where people can fall over them.
   - Clear up any spillages at once.
   - Watch where the leads for electrical tools are running and keep them away from heat and sharp edges.
   - Provide plenty of bags and boxes to keep small items and loose tools in.
4. Always tidy up the site at the end of the day. Don't leave flammable or toxic substances in open containers and sweep up all shavings and sawdust. Ensure that there are no live wires left exposed. Collect and lock away all tools and equipment out of reach of children.
5. One final point: any work which requires the stripping of materials containing asbestos should be done by a contractor licenced under the Asbestos (Licencing) Regulations 1983.

BANK

3 Looking after the money

Raising the finance

Before you carry out any repairs or improvements you must ask the questions 'Can I afford it?' and 'How can I pay for it?' Repairs to houses cost from 5p for a tap washer (if you do it yourself) to thousands of pounds for major roof repairs which would normally be carried out by a contractor. Home improvements are usually not as urgent as repairs and can be planned in advance. If you use this book sensibly you should be able to assess the approximate cost of having the work carried out by a contractor or the cost of buying the materials if you decide to do it yourself, together with an assessment of how long it should take you to do the work.

It is at this stage that you should consider how to pay for it. For those who wish to use borrowed money the position has been made more expensive by the withdrawal, from April 1988, of Income Tax relief for interest on loans (including additions to existing loans) taken out to finance home improvements. Abuse of the relief was widespread with people using the loans to buy a car, go on holiday etc, and the genuine DIY householder is suffering because of it.

There is now no relief at all against tax for interest paid on home improvement loans which has considerably reduced the attraction of using borrowed money.

Suppose, for instance, you want to build an extension costing £10,000. You have got £10,000 invested at the best rate available – say 9%. Your Bank Manager says he will be happy to lend you £10,000 and since you are a good customer he will charge you only 16%. What would be the cheapest method of financing your project?

This depends on whether you pay tax and if so at what rate. Let us assume:

A pays no tax
B pays tax at 25%
C pays tax at 40%

The net income generated by £10,000 invested at 9% is:

	A	B	C
£10,000 @ 9%	900	900	900
Less Income Tax to pay	NIL	225	360
Net Income from investment	900	675	540

The first option is to realise the investment and use the money to build the extension. The net cost of this would be:

	A	B	C
Loss of Income from investment	900	675	540

The second option is to keep the investment against a rainy day and borrow the £10,000 offered by your Bank Manager. This would cost:

	A	B	C
Annual interest on loan of £10,000 at 16% (no tax relief due)	1,600	1,600	1,600
Less			
Net income from investment still held	900	675	540
Net cost	700	925	1,060

Only 'A', the non-taxpayer, is better off by borrowing the money, and, having such a low income, he is the least likely to persuade his Bank Manager to lend him the money.

Of course there may be good reasons why you want to keep your investment anyway and you can see how important it is to review the financial position at an early stage. Consider your income and future prospects, your outgoings and likely future commitments, also the availability of any savings. You might, for instance, decide to take half the cost from savings and borrow the rest, to break the project down and spread it over a longer period, to cut down on contract labour and so on. Remember also all the non-building costs – it greatly reduces the pleasure of a new sun lounge if you have not enough money left to furnish it!

If you do decide to borrow funds you can of course still go to your Building Society (or another one) and ask for a non-MIRAS loan (i.e. one with no Income Tax relief attached to it). Most banks and finance houses are also keen to lend money these days particularly to home-owners and if the amount is no more than about £5,000 you might be able to get an unsecured loan or an overdraft. The latter would normally be at a lower rate of interest than other forms of borrowing and deposits of wages or salary help to keep down the balance on which the interest is calculated. On the debit side, you would lose your 'free banking' facility on going into the red unless you had a special arrangement with your bank manager.

There are other sources of finance, such as private borrowing from friends or relations or using your credit card, but these are unsatisfactory for varying reasons and the ones listed should be tried first. If your present building society or another financial institution turns you down for a mortgage, second mortgage, personal loan or overdraft there must be something radically wrong with your proposal which would make it almost certainly unacceptable to alternative sources of lending unless a very high rate of interest was charged.

Grants

In some circumstances grants are available from local authorities for house repairs and improvements. There are four types of grant and some brief notes are set out below to explain them but if you think you qualify you should contact the Improvement Grant Officer at your local authority for a leaflet containing full details. You should note that although the grants are standard some of the rules governing them vary in different local authorities.

Intermediate grant

This grant is available for houses built before 1901 and is concerned with the provision of basic amenities; you have the right to it (as opposed to its being at the discretion of the local authority) if you satisfy certain conditions. These amenities are:

(*a*) fixed bathroom or shower;
(*b*) wash-hand basin;
(*c*) sink;
(*d*) water closet;
(*e*) hot and cold water supply to amenities in this list.

It should be noted that the above amenities are only eligible for this grant if being provided for the first time (or have been missing for 12 months). In addition certain other associated works also qualify, e.g. drainage, repairs and decorating, other installation of some or all of above, the transfer of a bath from kitchen or scullery to bathroom, alterations to gas, electric or water services to accommodate the new amenities and also essential repairs. The grant payable is a percentage based upon the following eligible expenses limits:

	Greater London	Elsewhere
1. Fixed bath or shower	£590	£450
(a) hot and cold water	£750	£570
2. Wash-hand basin	£230	£170
(a) hot and cold water	£390	£305
3. Sink	£590	£450
(a) hot and cold water	£500	£385
4. Water closet	£890	£680
5. Repairs necessary to put building into reasonable state of repair	£4850	£3450
6. Reduced scale of repairs		
£345 per amenity up to maximum of		£1380
£485 per amenity up to maximum of	£1930	

The grant available is for 75% of the approved works (90% in cases of hardship).

Improvement grant

This grant is generally applicable to houses built before 1 January 1919 except in special cases where the date is 2 October 1961 the local authority must be satisfied that the work being carried out will enable the house to remain habitable for a long period. In most cases at least 50% of the work being carried out must come under the heading of 'improvements'. 'Repairs' will also be paid for but usually to support the improvements being carried out. (The 'repairs' section may be increased to 70% if the house is in a particularly bad state.) Defining what are improvements is difficult and you should seek guidance from your local Improvement Grant Officer.

In general terms he will be seeking to ensure that after the work is completed the property will conform to the following ten point standard:

(*a*) be substantially free from damp;
(*b*) have adequate natural lighting and ventilation in each habitable room;

(*c*) have adequate and safe provision throughout for artificial lighting, and have sufficient electric socket outlets for the safe and proper functioning of domestic appliances;
(*d*) be provided with adequate drainage facilities;
(*e*) be in a stable structural condition;
(*f*) have satisfactory internal arrangement;
(*g*) have satisfactory facilities for preparing and cooking food;
(*h*) be provided with adequate facilities for heating;
(*i*) have proper provision for the storage of fuel (where necessary) and for the storage of refuse;
(*j*) have in the roof space thermal insulation sufficient to give for the relevant structure a 'U' value of 0.35 W/m^2 °C. ('U' value defines how much heat will pass through a material. The lower the figure, the more heat is retained).

Repair grant

Only houses built before 1 January 1919 are eligible for this grant and the repairs necessary must be of a structural nature and have a minimum value of £2,400. The rateable value of property in the case of owner occupiers must be less than £226 (£400 in Greater London). The grant available is based upon a percentage of the maximum eligible expense limit of £4,800 and would normally cover such items as:

(*a*) roofs – replacing and repairing defective roofs and timbers and ancillary works;
(*b*) external walls – renewing or repairing defective walls, doors, windows, and damp proof courses;
(*c*) foundations – repair or renewal or underpinning;
(*d*) floors – repair or replacement;
(*e*) internal works – repair or replacement of walls, ceilings or staircases.

75% of the value of the work is the normal grant but it could be increased to 90% in cases of hardship.

Special grant

Owners of houses which have been converted into flats where tenants who are not members of the same family are sharing facilities, may be entitled to a special grant for the provision of separate basic amenities. Providing means of escape from fire can also qualify for this grant together with the associated repair works.

This grant is at the discretion of the local authority but would become mandatory if the council has served a notice on you under Section 15 of the Housing Act 1961 or Schedule 24 of the Housing Act 1980. In either case the grant would be 75% (20% in Greater London) of the approved cost of the works (90% in cases of hardship, except Greater London) up to a maximum eligible expense limit of £10,500 (£14,000 in Greater London) for the means of escape from fire and £3,450 for associated repairs (£4,850 in Greater London). The provision of basic amenities to the flats would be dealt with in the same manner as described under the Intermediate Grant rules.

There are special rules applicable to disabled people and also for listed buildings and you should ask your local authority for further information.

VAT and the DIY builder

Some explanation of the terms used in the tax is necessary first:

Zero-rating Any job which is 'zero-rated' does not suffer VAT and any VAT paid on supplies of goods or labour can be reclaimed from the Customs and Excise.

Standard-rating Any job which is 'standard-rated' suffers tax at the current rate (at present 15%) and any tax paid on supplies of goods and labour cannot be reclaimed.

Domestic construction work may fall into either category. Broadly, the construction of new buildings is zero-rated and all other types of work are standard rated.

The construction of new domestic buildings

This would include, for example, building a new house or bungalow, but if the new building is being erected on the remains of an old one then a very fine line is drawn between what is a new building which qualifies for 'zero-rating' and what is the re-construction of an old one which does not.

For example the following would qualify as new buildings:

(*a*) The construction of a building making use of a part or all of the foundations of an existing building, where the whole of the former building has been demolished to foundation level.

(*b*) The construction of a building making use of what remains of an existing building where this is limited to a single wall such as the front facade, or to a single wall plus all or part of the foundations, or to a single continuous facade covering two walls on a corner site.
(*c*) Building-on to an existing house to form two semi-detached houses without internal access to the existing building, and where planning permission etc. does not prevent its separate use, letting or disposal. The new building must stand on its own land.
(*d*) The building of a new house within an existing terrace of houses on the site of a house that has been totally demolished ('infilling').

The following do NOT qualify as the construction of a new building:

(*a*) The conversion, reconstruction, alteration or enlargement of an existing building or an extension or annexe which has internal access to the existing building.
(*b*) Where the outer walls of an existing building remain even without floor or roof; or where internal features are retained in addition to any part of the external wall structure.
(*c*) The building of an additional flat on top of an existing block.

A new detached garage would qualify for zero-rating if constructed at the same time as the house but not otherwise. Greenhouses, garden sheds are always standard rated.

If you are building a new house for yourself and you think your work will qualify for zero-rating call at the local VAT office (you will find the address under Customs & Excise in the Telephone Directory) and ask for Notice 719 "VAT Refunds for 'do-it-yourself' house builders" and Leaflet 708/2/87 'Construction Industry'. These will tell you what you can and cannot claim for and also how and when to claim.

Zero-rating also applies to certain work, goods and services provided on or for protected buildings and handicapped persons, details may be found in VAT Leaflets 708/1 and 701/7 respectively.

Insurance

The vast majority of home improvement work is successfully completed without a thought being given to the need for insurance cover, but there could be financial loss if you or a member of the public were injured as a result of your project.

If you intend to engage a contractor to do some of the work you should be certain that he has adequate Public Liability insurance to cover, for example, accidental injury to passers by, or the ruining of their clothes due to paint splashes. Ask your contractor if he has an Inland Revenue '714 Certificate'. If he has, he will also have the necessary Public Liability cover for this is a condition for issue of the certificate. If he is not a 714 certificate holder ask to see evidence of current Public Liability insurance before accepting any estimate he has submitted.

For those who are building a house or bungalow for their own occupation with the help of employees and/or labour only subcontractors at least one Insurance Company (Norwich Union) has a 'self build' Insurance Policy. This covers:

Employer's Liability	– injury to an employee or labour-only sub-contractor
Public Liability	– injury to members of the public (the limit may be £500,000 or £1,000,000 for any one accident)
Contract Works	– (a) 'All risks' covered – loss or damage to the building and materials on site or in transit. (b) Plant, tools, and equipment up to £2,000. (c) Employees personal effects – up to £200 any one employee.

There is a £100 excess under (a) and (b) and a £15 excess under (c). The insurance is not available for the extension, alteration, repair or renovation of existing buildings.

A general Personal Accident or sickness policy which provides for weekly payments during temporary disablement as well as lump sums for more serious injuries is a useful safeguard, but do ensure that the type of activity you are proposing to undertake is covered before you pay the premium.

Don't forget, these prices may need adjustment depending on where you live.
Regional adjustments are provided on the inside cover, and further explanation is given in the Preface.

WIRING & INSTALLING
LAMPS
CEILING
TILING
TO INSTALLING HOOD
DOUBLE GLAZING
CUPBOARDS
CUPBOARDS INSTALLING
TILING

4 Assessing the cost

In this chapter information on hours and costs is given under various headings. To find out the total cost or number of hours for a particular job, however, you need to add up the various amounts set against the relevant descriptions. For example, if you intend to take out a fireplace consisting of a tiled concrete surround and hearth and then brick up the opening, plaster the new brickwork and fix a length of timber skirting, you would need to collect the hours and costs in the second, third and fourth descriptions under Fireplaces below. This concept of collecting information from more than one description to build up a composite value or number of hours applies throughout the book.

Disposal of rubbish

The items for demolitions, alteration work, putting down, breaking out and excavation in this book do not include for the cost of removing debris or excavated material. There are two ways of doing this, loading into skips or loading into lorries. It is unlikely that a householder would become involved in the hiring of lorries so only the skip option is considered. Assuming the skips would be loaded to capacity the costs should be:

Size of skip	Daily hire rate £	Cost per m or yd £
3 cu yd	14.55	4.85
6 cu yd	32.00	5.33
8 cu yd	36.80	4.60
3 cu m	17.00	5.66
6 cu m	34.50	5.75
8 cu m	39.10	4.89

Load debris into wheelbarrow, wheel average 25 m deposit in skip	1 cu yd	1:05	–	1	5.85
	1 cu m	1:15	–	1	4.90
Cost of removal of debris in 6 cu m or yd skip (including tipping charges)	1 cu yd	–	–	–	5.33
	1 cu m	–	–	–	5.75

You should remember that the above figures apply only to full loads. Hiring a skip and only half filling it would be a more expensive business per unit.

If for some other reason you wished to hire a lorry it should cost you approximately £20 per hour for lorry and driver, but bear in mind that the minimum hire period would probably be half a day, i.e. £80.

Don't forget, these prices may need adjustment depending on where you live.
Regional adjustments are provided on the inside cover, and further explanation is given in the Preface.

Treatment of timber

It is estimated that more than 75% of the houses in Britain suffer from insect infestation, the most common being the furniture beetle. Most of the damage they cause is of a minor nature and is confined to unpainted surfaces but if they attack structural timbers, action should be taken immediately. Professional help should be sought but in straightforward cases of minor infestation (or preventative action) the following information should be of use. It is assumed that the insecticidal wood preserver will be applied by brush and that gaining access to the areas requiring treatment is not difficult.

Apply one coat insecticidal wood preserver on					
general surfaces	1 sq yd (1 sq m)	0:15 (0:17)	0.10 (0.12)	2	2.00 (2.20)

If you decided to use spraying equipment instead of brushing, the hire cost of the equipment is £18.50 for the first day, £9.25 for each subsequent day or £37 for a week.

Damp treatment

There are two main types of dampness in buildings – penetrating and rising damp. Penetrating damp can be observed by patches of dampness on the external walls and is usually caused by one of the following:

1. Cracked or porous brickwork.
2. Defective rendering or pointing.
3. Damaged flashing.
4. Leaking gutter or rainwater pipe.
5. Bridged cavity.

Here are some costs and hours associated with this work.

Cut out single brick and replace with new in external wall and bed and point in cement mortar	1 no	1:00	0.60	4	6.60
Hack off defective rendering and renew in one coat cement mortar	1 sq yd (1 sq m)	2:20 (2:50)	1.50 (1.80)	5	10.00 (12.00)
Rake out joints of existing mortar and point up in cement mortar	1 sq yd (1 sq m)	1:50 (2:10)	0.30 (0.35)	5	8.40 10.00
Rake out horizontal joint in wall, refix flashing and point up in cement mortar	1 yd (1 m)	0:40 (0:45)	0.55 (0.60)	5	3.50 4.00
Rake out horizontal joint in wall, refix stepped flashing and point up in cement mortar	1 yd (1 m)	0:50 (0:55)	0.55 (0.60)	5	4.30 4.75
Remove 6 ft length of existing rainwater gutter and replace with new gutter					
4½″ (110 mm) half round cast iron	1 no	2:00	10.35	5	25. 00
4½″ (110 mm) half round plastic	1 no	1:30	4.20	5	15.00

Remove 6 ft length of existing rainwater pipe and replace with new pipe					
3″ (75 mm) diameter cast iron	1 no	1:50	15.50	5	26.00
2½″ (68 mm) diameter plastic	1 no	1:00	4.20	5	11.00
Remove 6 bricks from external leaf of cavity wall, inspect and remove mortar from wall tie, reset bricks and point up	1 no	3:00	0.80	5	25.00

Rising damp is usually caused by a defective or non-existent damp proof course (dpc). There are various methods of inserting a dpc into an existing wall but injecting a chemical waterproofing liquid is probably the most effective one within the range of skills of the DIY enthusiast. The method consists of drilling a series of holes 4½″ (112 mm) apart and pumping in the fluid which permeates the brickwork.

The cost of hiring the equipment is £18.50 for the first day and £9.25 for each subsequent day or £37 for a week. The cost of hiring a drill (¾″ to 1″ chuck) is £7, £9 and £18 respectively. The following reflect the labour and waterproofing liquid costs for treating one face of an external wall.

Drill holes ¾″ (18 mm) diameter, 3″ (75 mm) deep at 4½″ (110 mm) centres, inject chemical dpc and make good holes	1 yd (1 m)	3:00 (3:60)	6.50 (7.80)	5	20.00 24.00

The plaster must be hacked off from the internal face of the wall and the skirting removed before the work commences and renewed on completion.

Hack off existing plaster 3 ft (1 m) high and replaster	1 yd (1 m)	2:20 (2:35)	2.10 (2.30)	7	12.00 13.00
Take off existing skirting and renew with 4″ (100 mm) high painted softwood skirting	1 yd (1 m)	0:36 (0:43)	1.28 (1.50)	5	3.75 4.50

Fireplaces

The removal and replacement of fireplaces is a task that can be tackled by most DIY enthusiasts – provided they have enough muscle to remove the debris! Unless the old fireplace can be broken up indoors, which is not usually desirable, some help will be required. The DIY hours shown below are for the total man hours necessary to complete the work. The scrap (or antique) value of the fireplace has been ignored. No allowance has been made for removing debris (see p.47).

Take out timber fireplace surround size					
3′6″ × 3′0″ (1050 × 900 mm)	1 no	1:00	–	3	6.00
4′0″ × 3′6″ (1200 × 1050 mm)	1 no	1:05	–	3	8.00
5′0″ × 4′0″ (1500 × 1200 mm)	1 no	1:10	–	3	10.00
Take out tiled concrete fireplace surround size					
3′6″ × 3′0″ (1050 × 900 mm)	1 no	2:00	–	3	12.00
4′0″ × 3′6″ (1200 × 1050 mm)	1 no	2:30	–	3	17.00
5′0″ × 4′0″ (1500 × 1200 mm)	1 no	3:00	–	3	22.00
Take out tiled concrete or stone hearth size					
3′6″ × 1′6″ (1050 × 450 mm)	1 no	1:00	–	3	8.00
3′6″ × 2′0″ (1050 × 600 mm)	1 no	1:20	–	3	9.00
4′0″ × 2′0″ (1200 × 600 mm)	1 no	1:30	–	3	9.00
5′0″ × 3′0″ (1500 × 900 mm)	1 no	2:30	–	3	17.00
Brick up opening size 1′6″ × 2′0″ high (450 × 600 mm) after removal of fireplace, patch plaster walls, fix new skirting 6″ high (150 mm) across opening	1 no	8:00	14.00	5	38.00

The following prices indicate the time and cost involved in fixing new fireplaces. Due to the wide range of products the information has been based upon the basic price of a selection of fireplaces.

Fix new fireplace after removal of existing one (see above) including patch plastering around edges					
Basic price – £100	1 no	6:00	105.00	3	130.00
Basic price – £150	1 no	6:00	155.00	3	190.00
Basic price – £200	1 no	6:00	205.00	3	230.00

Don't forget, these prices may need adjustment depending on where you live.
Regional adjustments are provided on the inside cover, and further explanation is given in the Preface.

External wall treatment and chimney pots

Repairs

The following information relates to the sundry repair and re-pointing of existing brickwork and the replacement of defective chimney pots. It is necessary to re-point old brickwork in order to prevent infiltration of dampness caused by driving rain or leaking pipework penetrating the decayed mortar. Apart from fulfilling this important functional need, re-pointing also improves the appearance of a building. The figures quoted below refer to work carried out at ground level and 20% should be added to the hours and costs for work executed from ladders and 10% from platforms.

Rake out joints of existing brickwork and point up in cement mortar	1 sq yd (1 sq m)	1:50 (2:10)	0.30 (0.35)	5	8.40 (10.00)
Cut out single brick from external wall and replace with new set in cement mortar	1 no	1:00	0.60	4	3.70
Cut out terra cotta air brick size 9″ × 3″ (220 × 75 mm) and replace with new set in cement mortar	1 no	1:00	2.50	4	5.40

Chimney pots

In the case of the replacement of chimney pots the question of access is critical. The cost of erecting scaffolding and secure walkways to the stack would normally far exceed the cost for the work to be done. It may be possible to gain access to the stack from a rooflight which would reduce the cost considerably. Because of these uncertainties the following costs and hours represent the cost of carrying out the work only and not the cost of the scaffolding or towers.

Remove existing defective chimney pot, hack away flaunching, fix new terra cotta pot 8″ diameter × 12″ high (185 × 300 mm) and set in cement mortar	1 no	4:00	11.50	4	35.00
As above but 1′6″ (450 mm) high	1 no	4:30	13.25	4	40.00

Roofing

The skills required to carry out roof repairs can vary enormously. Sometimes the repair work is straightforward but gaining safe and secure access can be difficult and in these circumstances you would be better to call in a contractor. This section is divided into three parts – repairs to pitched roofs involving slates and tiles; repairs to flat roofs covered in bituminous roofing felt; and new work. The cost of removing debris is not included in the following costs nor is the cost of hiring any specialist equipment such as roof ladders.

Remember that as explained in Chapter 1 the contractor's cost only reflects the cost of carrying out the work and not the travelling. Although the cost is given at £9.00 for a contractor to refix one slate, he may charge considerably more when he adds on his travelling time and costs.

Repairs to pitched roofs

Take up covering from pitched roof for disposal					
tiles	1 sq yd (1 sq m)	0:40 (0:45)	–	3	3.50 (4.20)
slates	1 sq yd (1 sq m)	0:40 (0:45)	–	3	3.50 (4.20)
timber boarding	1 sq yd (1 sq m)	0:50 (1:00)	–	3	4.30 (5.15)
battens	1 sq yd (1 sq m)	0:10 (0:12)	–	3	0.80 (1.00)
underfelt	1 sq yd (1 sq m)	0:05 (0:07)	–	3	0.40 (0.50)
flat sheeting	1 sq yd (1 sq m)	0:15 (0:20)	–	3	1.40 (1.70)
corrugated sheeting	1 sq yd (1 sq m)	0:13 (0:20)	–	3	1.40 (1.70)

Carefully take up covering from pitched roof and lay aside for re-use					
tiles	1 sq yd	1:00	–	3	4.00
	(1 sq m)	(1:20)			(4.80)
slates	1 sq yd	1:00	–	3	4.00
	(1 sq m)	(1:20)			(4.80)
timber boarding	1 sq yd	1:20	–	3	5.50
	(1 sq m)	(1:40)			(6.60)
flat sheeting	1 sq yd	0:35	–	3	1.80
	(1 sq m)	(0:40)			(2.20)
corrugated sheeting	1 sq yd	0:35	–	3	1.80
	(1 sq m)	(0:40)			(2.20)
Remove single broken slate, replace with slate laid aside previously	1 no	1:10	–	6	9.00
Remove single broken slate and replace with new Welsh blue slate size					
1′8″ × 10″ (500 × 250 mm)	1 no	1:10	1.75	6	10.50
2′0″ × 1′0″ (600 × 300 mm)	1 no	1:10	2.75	6	11.50
Remove slates from area not exceeding 1 sq yd (1 sq m) and replace with new Welsh blue slate size					
1′8″ × 10″ (500 × 250 mm)	1 sq yd	3:00	25.00	6	50.00
	(1 sq m)	(3:40)	(30.00)		(60.00)
2′0″ × 1′0″ (600 × 300 mm)	1 sq yd	2:30	31.00	6	47.00
	(1 sq m)	(3:00)	(38.00)		(56.00)
Remove single broken tile, replace with tile previously laid aside	1 no	1:00	–	6	8.00
Remove single broken tile replace with new					
plain tile size 10½″ × 6½″ (265 × 165 mm)	1 no	1:00	0.25	6	7.50
interlocking tile size 1′4½″ × 1′1″ (410 × 330 mm)	1 no	1:00	0.60	6	9.00

Take off defective ridge or hip cappings and re-set in cement mortar	1 yd (1 m)	1:30 (1:40)	0.20 (0.25)	4	8.80 (10.50)
Take off defective ridge or hip cappings and replace with new bed and point in cement mortar	1 yd (1 m)	1:10 (1:20)	3.00 (3.30)	4	10.00 (12.00)

Repairs to flat roofs

Repairs to built up bituminous felt roofing should only be carried out by an amateur if they are of a minor nature such as small cracks or blisters. If the surface is in poor condition or if there is a profusion of defects it is better to call in a contractor to re-roof the whole surface.

Cut out crack in bituminous felt roofing, apply bituminous compound and apply sealing tape 6″ wide (150 mm)	1 yd (1 m)	1:00 (1:10)	1.80 (2.00)	5	5.00 (6.00)
Cut out blister in bituminous felt roofing, apply bituminous compound and apply sealing tape to area approximately 12″ × 12″ (300 × 300 mm)	1 no	0:50 (0:55)	1.30 (1.45)	5	4.00 (4.80)

New roof coverings

The laying of pitched and flat roof coverings is a job for the expert and the following information should give you an indication of what you would expect to pay. Note that the extra items involved in roofing, e.g. extra courses of tiles at verges and eaves, flashings,

Don't forget, these prices may need adjustment depending on where you live.
Regional adjustments are provided on the inside cover, and further explanation is given in the Preface.

underfelt and battens (where applicable) have been allowed for in the overall rate.

Description	Quantity	Contractor's price £
Roofing felt	1 sq yd (1 sq m)	2.00 (2.40)
1″ (25 mm) tongued and grooved softwood boarding	1 sq yd (1 sq m)	13.00 (15.60)
2″ (50 mm) wood wool slabs (unreinforced)	1 sq yd (1 sq m)	12.00 (14.40)
Welsh blue slates size		
1′8″ × 10″ (500 × 250 mm)	1 sq yd (1 sq m)	40.00 (48.00)
2′0″ × 1′0″ (600 × 300 mm)	1 sq yd (1 sq m)	40.00 (48.00)
Plain concrete tile size 10½″ × 6½″ (265 × 165 mm)	1 sq yd (1 sq m)	27.00 (36.00)
Interlocking tile size 1′4½″ × 1′1″ (410 × 330 mm)	1 sq yd (1 sq m)	16.00 (19.20)
Bituminous fibre-based built up roofing with top layer mineral surface		
two layer	1 sq yd (1 sq m)	8.00 (9.60)
three layer	1 sq yd (1 sq m)	12.00 (14.40)
Bituminous asbestos-based built up roofing with top layer mineral surface		
two layer	1 sq yd (1 sq m)	12.00 (14.40)
three layer	1 sq yd (1 sq m)	16.00 (19.20)

Doors

Fitting a new door either because of damage or to improve a room's appearance can make a significant improvement for only a few hours work. Although there are a multitude of doors on the market there are only five main types:

Panelled	these are traditional doors where panels are set into a surrounding frame;
Flush	most post-war buildings contain flush doors;
Glazed	these are normally used where there is a need for light, e.g. in a corridor or an entrance;
Ledged and braced	these doors are the least attractive (although not necessarily the cheapest) and are used in situations where appearance is not the main consideration, e.g. a yard entrance or an outhouse;
Period doors	these are made from hardwood and usually incorporate panels or fanlights to give a Tudor or Georgian appearance and are mainly used as front entrance doors.

Removing doors, frames and ironmongery

Take off existing door					
internal	1 no	0:30	–	3	1.50
external	1 no	0:40	–	3	2.00
Take out existing door frame or lining	1 no	0:40	–	3	2.00
Take off existing ironmongery					
bolt	1 no	0:10	–	3	1.00
deadlock	1 no	0:20	–	3	1.50
mortice lock	1 no	0:15	–	3	1.50
mortice latch	1 no	0:15	–	3	1.50
cylinder lock	1 no	0:15	–	3	1.50
door closer	1 no	0:15	–	3	1.50

Exterior flush for painting

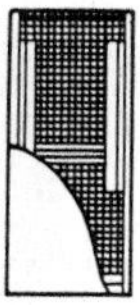
CF1X

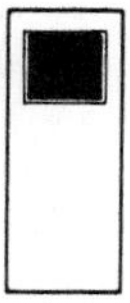
■ CF2X

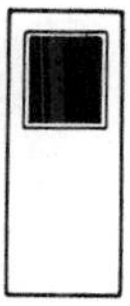
■ CF3X

■ CF4X

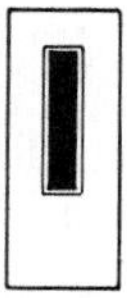
■ CF14X

Moulded and embossed

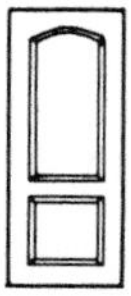
Classique

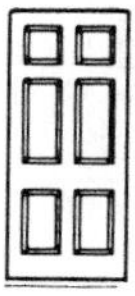
Colonist

Heritage

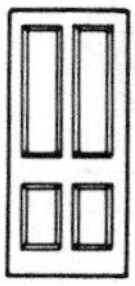
Wordsworth

Garage redwood

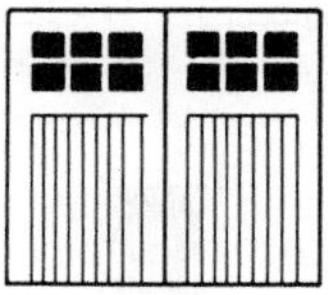
CGG

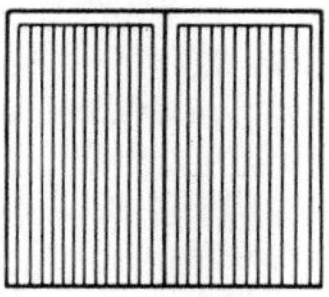
CGP

Period Brazilian mahogany

Portcullis Beaded

Gothic Half Light

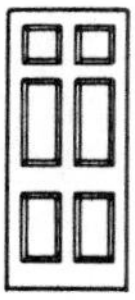
6 Panel

4 Panel

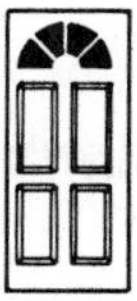
4 Panel Fanlight

Tudor

Knightsbridge

Half Bow

Kentucky

Chelsea

Casement and panel

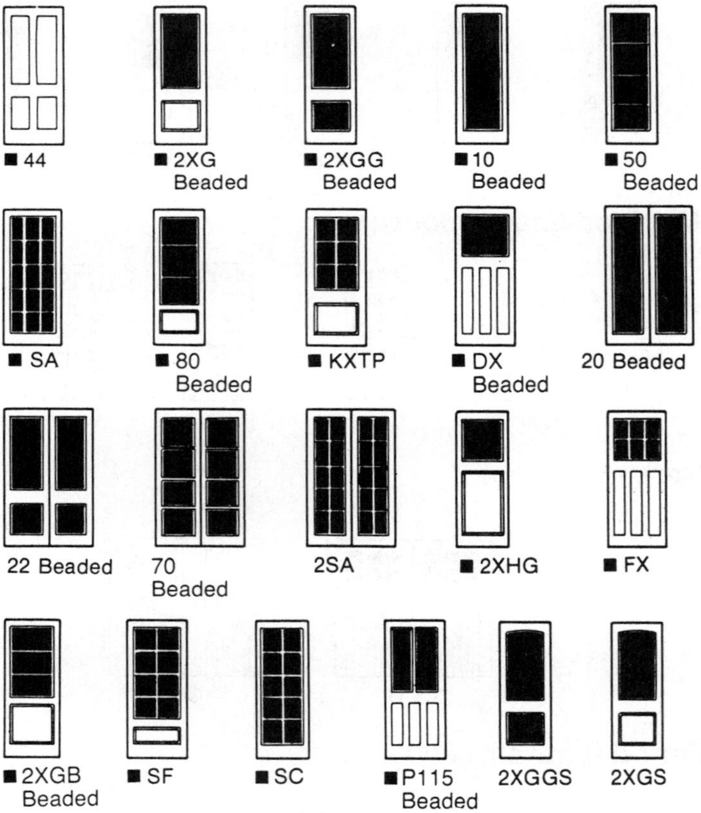

■ 44
■ 2XG Beaded
■ 2XGG Beaded
■ 10 Beaded
■ 50 Beaded
■ SA
■ 80 Beaded
■ KXTP
■ DX Beaded
20 Beaded
22 Beaded
70 Beaded
2SA
■ 2XHG
■ FX
■ 2XGB Beaded
■ SF
■ SC
■ P115 Beaded
2XGGS
2XGS

Marlborough softwood

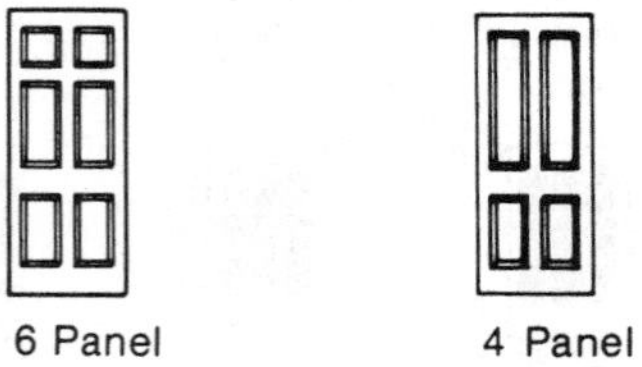

6 Panel
4 Panel

Period Canadian softwood

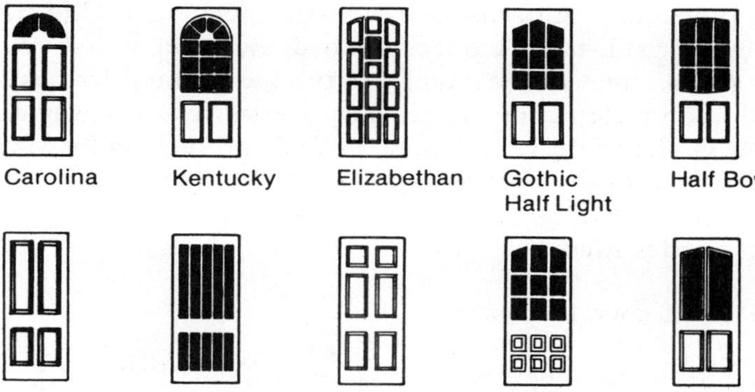
Carolina
Kentucky
Elizabethan
Gothic Half Light
Half Bow
4 Panel
Portcullis Beaded
6 Panel
Knightsbridge
Chelsea

Period red meranti

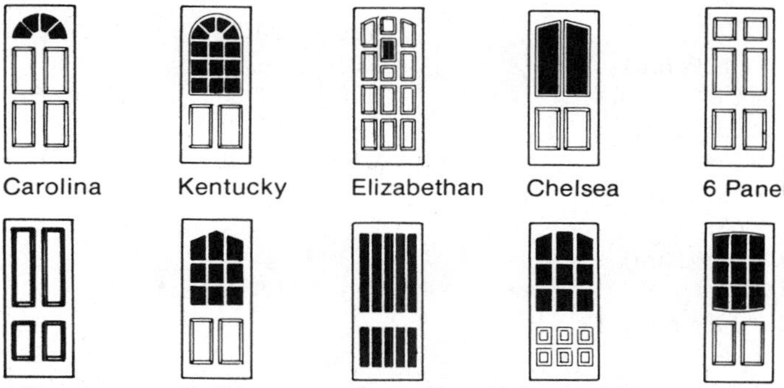
Carolina
Kentucky
Elizabethan
Chelsea
6 Panel
4 Panel
Gothic Half Light
Portcullis Beaded
Knightsbridge
Half Bow

Panel and casement meranti

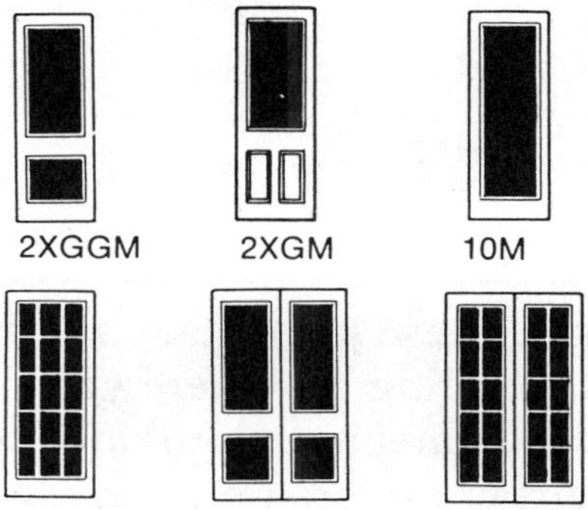
2XGGM
2XGM
10M
SAM
22M
2SAM

There are many types of doors available and the following are based upon products manufactured by Messrs Crosby Door Ltd, Groundwall Industrial Estate, Stephenson Road, Swindon, Wiltshire and the trade names refer to their range of products. The prices have been based upon information supplied by Messrs W.F. Hollway and Bros Ltd, 42 Grafton Street, Liverpool, L8 5SF and include for VAT.

Apart from flush doors most doors are sold by a standard reference code or name and the previous three pages of diagrams illustrate the various codes used.

Interior flush doors for painting

These doors are usually unprimed unless you specifically order otherwise

1⅜″ (35 mm) thick hardboard finish door					
2′0″ × 6′0″ (610 × 1829 mm)	1 no	1:30	18.20	6	30.00
1′3″ × 6′6″ (381 × 1981 mm)	1 no	1:30	18.20	6	30.00
1′6″ × 6′6″ (457 × 1981 mm)	1 no	1:30	18.20	6	30.00
1′9″ × 6′6″ (533 × 1981 mm)	1 no	1:30	18.20	6	30.00
2′0″ × 6′6″ (610 × 1981 mm)	1 no	1:30	18.20	6	30.00
2′3″ × 6′6″ (686 × 1981 mm)	1 no	1:30	18.20	6	30.00
2′4″ × 6′6″ (711 × 1981 mm)	1 no	1:30	18.20	6	30.00
2′6″ × 6′6″ (762 × 1981 mm)	1 no	1:30	18.20	6	30.00
2′8″ × 6′8″ (813 × 2032 mm)	1 no	1:30	19.02	6	32.00
2′9″ × 6′6″ (838 x 1981 mm)	1 no	1:30	19.02	6	32.00

Don't forget, these prices may need adjustment depending on where you live.

Regional adjustments are provided on the inside cover, and further explanation is given in the Preface.

1⅜″ (35 mm) thick unlipped 'Primaseal' door					
1′3″ × 6′6″ (381 × 1981 mm)	1 no	1:30	17.30	6	29.00
1′6″ × 6′6″ (457 × 1981 mm)	1 no	1:30	17.30	6	29.00
1′9″ × 6′6″ (533 × 1981 mm)	1 no	1:30	17.30	6	29.00
2′0″ × 6′6″ (610 × 1981 mm)	1 no	1:30	17.30	6	29.00
2′3″ × 6′6″ (686 × 1981 mm)	1 no	1:30	17.30	6	29.00
2′4″ × 6′4″ (711 × 1930 mm)	1 no	1:30	17.30	6	29.00
2′4″ × 6′6″ (711 × 1981 mm)	1 no	1:30	17.30	6	29.00
2′6″ × 6′6″ (762 × 1981 mm)	1 no	1:30	17.30	6	29.00
2′8″ × 6′8″ (813 × 2032 mm)	1 no	1:30	18.10	6	31.00
2′9″ × 6′6″ (838 × 1981 mm)	1 no	1:30	18.10	6	31.00
1⅜″ (35 mm) thick 'Paintply' door					
2′0″ × 6′0″ (610 × 1829 mm)	1 no	1:30	23.65	6	36.00
1′3″ × 6′6″ (381 × 1981 mm)	1 no	1:30	23.65	6	36.00
1′6″ × 6′6″ (457 × 1981 mm)	1 no	1:30	23.65	6	36.00
1′9″ × 6′6″ (533 × 1981 mm)	1 no	1:30	23.65	6	36.00
2′0″ × 6′6″ (610 × 1981 mm)	1 no	1:30	23.65	6	36.00
2′3″ × 6′6″ (686 × 1981 mm)	1 no	1:30	23.65	6	36.00
2′4″ × 6′4″ (711 × 1930 mm)	1 no	1:30	23.65	6	36.00
2′4″ × 6′6″ (711 × 1981 mm)	1 no	1:30	23.65	6	36.00
2′6″ × 6′6″ (762 × 1981 mm)	1 no	1:30	23.65	6	36.00

2′8″ × 6′8″ (813 × 2032 mm)	1 no	1:30	24.70	6	37.00
2′9″ × 6′6″ (838 × 1981 mm)	1 no	1:30	24.90	6	37.00
1⅝″ (40 mm) thick 'Paintply' door					
1′6″ × 6′6″ (457 × 1981 mm)	1 no	1:30	24.50	6	37.00
1′9″ × 6′6″ (533 × 1981 mm)	1 no	1:30	24.50	6	37.00
2′0″ × 6′6″ (610 × 1981 mm)	1 no	1:30	24.50	6	37.00
2′3″ × 6′6″ (686 × 1981 mm)	1 no	1:30	24.50	6	37.00
2′6″ × 6′6″ (762 × 1981 mm)	1 no	1:30	24.50	6	37.00
2′8″ × 6′8″ (813 × 2032 mm)	1 no	1:30	25.70	6	38.00
2′9″ × 6′6″ (838 × 1981 mm)	1 no	1:30	25.80	6	38.00

Interior flush doors factory finished

These doors come self finished and only require waxing or polishing to enhance their appearance

1⅜″ (35 mm) thick select de luxe 'Scyntilla' sapele door					
1′6″ × 6′6″ (457 × 1981 mm)	1 no	1:30	30.70	6	43.00
1′9″ × 6′6″ (533 × 1981 mm)	1 no	1:30	30.70	6	43.00
2′0″ × 6′6″ (610 × 1981 mm)	1 no	1:30	30.70	6	43.00
2′3″ × 6′6″ (686 × 1981 mm)	1 no	1:30	30.70	6	43.00
2′6″ × 6′6″ (762 × 1981 mm)	1 no	1:30	30.70	6	43.00
2′8″ × 6′8″ (813 × 2032 mm)	1 no	1:30	32.30	6	45.00
2′9″ × 6′6″ (838 × 1981 mm)	1 no	1:30	32.40	6	45.00

1⅜″ (35 mm) thick de luxe 'Scyntilla' Okoume/Makore/Koto door					
2′0″ × 6′6″ (610 × 1981 mm)	1 no	1:30	39.40	6	52.00
2′3″ × 6′6″ (686 × 1981 mm)	1 no	1:30	35.00	6	48.00
2′6″ × 6′6″ (762 × 1981 mm)	1 no	1:30	35.00	6	48.00
2′9″ × 6′6″ (838 × 1981 mm)	1 no	1:30	36.60	6	50.00
1⅜″ (35 mm) thick sapele 'Scyntilla' door					
1′3″ × 6′6″ (381 × 1981 mm)	1 no	1:30	26.60	6	38.00
1′6″ × 6′6″ (457 × 1981 mm)	1 no	1:30	26.60	6	38.00
1′9″ × 6′6″ (522 × 1981 mm)	1 no	1:30	26.60	6	38.00
2′0″ × 6′6″ (610 × 1981 mm)	1 no	1:30	26.60	6	38.00
2′3″ x 6′6″ (686 × 1981 mm)	1 no	1:30	26.60	6	38.00
2′6″ × 6′6″ (762 × 1981 mm)	1 no	1:30	26.60	6	38.00
2′8″ × 6′8″ (813 × 2032 mm)	1 no	1:30	26.60	6	38.00
2′9″ × 6′6″ (838 × 1981 mm)	1 no	1:30	26.60	6	38.00
1⅜″ (35 mm) thick de luxe teak 'Scyntilla' door					
2′0″ × 6′6″ (610 × 1981 mm)	1 no	1:30	57.50	6	75.00
2′3″ × 6′6″ (686 × 1981 mm)	1 no	1:30	57.50	6	75.00
2′6″ × 6′6″ (762 × 1981 mm)	1 no	1:30	57.50	6	75.00

1⅜″ (35 mm) thick de luxe oak 'Scyntilla' door					
2′0″ × 6′6″ (610 × 1981 mm)	1 no	1:30	57.50	6	75.00
2′3″ × 6′6″ (686 × 1981 mm)	1 no	1:30	57.50	6	75.00
2′6″ × 6′6″ (762 × 1981 mm)	1 no	1:30	57.50	6	75.00
1⅝″ (40 mm) thick de luxe 'Scyntilla' Okoume/Makore/Koto door					
526 × 2040 mm	1 no	1:30	38.30	6	53.00
626 × 2040 mm	1 no	1:30	38.30	6	53.00
726 × 2040 mm	1 no	1:30	38.30	6	53.00
826 × 2040 mm	1 no	1:30	39.40	6	54.00
1⅝″ (40 mm) thick de luxe 'Scyntilla' Oak/Teak door					
526 × 2040 mm	1 no	1:30	58.70	6	75.00
626 × 2040 mm	1 no	1:30	58.70	6	75.00
726 × 2040 mm	1 no	1:30	58.70	6	75.00
826 × 2040 mm	1 no	1:30	59.20	6	77.00
1⅝″ (40 mm) thick de luxe sapele 'Scyntilla' door					
526 × 2040 mm	1 no	1:30	32.90	6	45.00
626 × 2040 mm	1 no	1:30	32.90	6	45.00
726 × 2040 mm	1 no	1:30	32.90	6	45.00
826 × 2040 mm	1 no	1:30	34.00	6	46.00
Moulded and embossed interior doors for painting					
1⅜″ (35 mm) thick 'Classique' door					
1′9″ × 6′6″ (533 × 1981 mm)	1 no	1:30	44.50	6	60.00
2′0″ × 6′6″ (610 × 1981 mm)	1 no	1:30	44.50	6	60.00
2′3″ × 6′6″ (686 × 1981 mm)	1 no	1:30	44.50	6	60.00
2′6″ × 6′6″ (762 × 1981 mm)	1 no	1:30	44.50	6	60.00

2′8″ × 6′8″ (813 × 2032 mm)	1 no	1:30	48.90	6	65.00
2′9″ × 6′6″ (838 × 1981 mm)	1 no	1:30	48.90	6	65.00
1⅜″ (35 mm) thick 'Colonist' door					
1′9″ × 6′6″ (533 × 1981 mm)	1 no	1:30	42.30	6	56.00
2′0″ × 6′6″ (610 × 1981 mm)	1 no	1:30	42.30	6	56.00
2′3″ × 6′6″ (686 × 1981 mm)	1 no	1:30	42.30	6	56.00
2′6″ × 6′6″ (762 × 1981 mm)	1 no	1:30	42.30	6	56.00
2′8″ × 6′8″ (813 × 2032 mm)	1 no	1:30	46.80	6	60.00
2′9″ × 6′6″ (838 × 1981 mm)	1 no	1:30	46.80	6	60.00
1⅜″ (35 mm) thick 'Heritage' door					
1′6″ × 6′6″ (457 × 1981 mm)	1 no	1:30	57.00	6	75.00
1′9″ × 6′6″ (533 × 1981 mm)	1 no	1:30	57.00	6	75.00
2′0″ × 6′6″ (610 × 1981 mm)	1 no	1:30	57.00	6	75.00
2′3″ × 6′6″ (686 × 1981 mm)	1 no	1:30	57.00	6	75.00
2′6″ × 6′6″ (762 × 1981 mm)	1 no	1:30	57.00	6	75.00
2′8″ × 6′8″ (813 × 2032 mm)	1 no	1:30	60.40	6	78.00
2′9″ × 6′6″ (838 × 1981 mm)	1 no	1:30	62.30	6	80.00

Don't forget, these prices may need adjustment depending on where you live.
Regional adjustments are provided on the inside cover, and further explanation is given in the Preface.

1⅜″ (35 mm) thick 'Wordsworth' door					
1′9″ × 6′6″ (533 × 1981 mm)	1 no	1:30	30.00	6	42.00
2′0″ × 6′6″ (610 × 1981 mm)	1 no	1:30	30.00	6	42.00
2′3″ × 6′6″ (686 × 1981 mm)	1 no	1:30	30.00	6	42.00
2′6″ × 6′6″ (762 × 1981 mm)	1 no	1:30	30.00	6	42.00
2′8″ × 6′8″ (813 × 2032 mm)	1 no	1:30	33.50	6	45.00
2′9″ × 6′6″ (838 × 1981 mm)	1 no	1:30	33.50	6	45.00
1⅝″ (40 mm) thick 'Classique' door					
626 × 2040 mm	1 no	1:30	48.70	6	62.00
726 × 2040 mm	1 no	1:30	48.70	6	62.00
826 × 2040 mm	1 no	1:30	49.70	6	64.00
1⅝″ (40 mm) thick 'Colonist' door					
626 × 2040 mm	1 no	1:30	45.10	6	60.00
726 × 2040 mm	1 no	1:30	45.10	6	60.00
826 × 2040 mm	1 no	1:30	46.00	6	62.00
1⅝″ (40 mm) thick 'Heritage' door					
626 × 2040 mm	1 no	1:30	58.20	6	75.00
726 × 2040 mm	1 no	1:30	58.20	6	75.00
826 × 2040 mm	1 no	1:30	59.20	6	77.00
1⅝″ (40 mm) thick 'Wordsworth' door					
626 × 2040 mm	1 no	1:30	31.70	6	45.00
726 × 2040 mm	1 no	1:30	31.70	6	45.00
826 × 2040 mm	1 no	1:30	33.50	6	48.00
Interior casement and panel doors					
1⅜″ (35 mm) thick door pattern 44					
2′0″ × 6′6″ (610 × 1981 mm)	1 no	1:30	77.80	6	100.00
2′3″ × 6′6″ (686 × 1981 mm)	1 no	1:30	77.80	6	100.00
2′6″ × 6′6″ (762 × 1981 mm)	1 no	1:30	77.80	6	100.00

1⅜″ (35 mm) thick door pattern 2XG with loose beads					
2′0″ × 6′6″ (610 × 1981 mm)	1 no	1:30	48.00	6	62.00
2′3″ × 6′6″ (686 × 1981 mm)	1 no	1:30	48.00	6	62.00
2′6″ × 6′6″ (762 × 1981 mm)	1 no	1:30	48.00	6	62.00
1⅜″ (35 mm) thick door pattern 2XGG with loose beads					
2′0″ × 6′6″ (610 × 1981 mm)	1 no	1:30	46.60	6	60.00
2′3″ × 6′6″ (686 × 1981 mm)	1 no	1:30	46.60	6	60.00
2′6″ × 6′6″ (762 × 1981 mm)	1 no	1:30	46.60	6	60.00
1⅜″ (35 mm) thick door pattern 10 with loose beads					
2′0″ × 6′6″ (610 × 1981 mm)	1 no	1:30	37.90	6	50.00
2′3″ × 6′6″ (686 × 1981 mm)	1 no	1:30	37.90	6	50.00
2′6″ × 6′6″ (762 × 1981 mm)	1 no	1:30	37.90	6	50.00
1⅜″ (35 mm) thick door pattern 50 with loose beads					
2′0″ × 6′6″ (610 × 1981 mm)	1 no	1:30	43.75	6	58.00
2′3″ × 6′6″ (686 × 1981 mm)	1 no	1:30	43.75	6	58.00
2′6″ × 6′6″ (762 × 1981 mm)	1 no	1:30	43.75	6	58.00
1⅜″ (35 mm) thick door pattern SA					
2′0″ × 6′6″ (610 × 1981 mm)	1 no	1:30	62.00	6	80.00
2′3″ × 6′6″ (686 × 1981 mm)	1 no	1:30	62.00	6	80.00
2′6″ × 6′6″ (762 × 1981 mm)	1 no	1:30	62.00	6	80.00

1⅜″ (35 mm) thick door pattern 80 with loose beads					
2′0″ × 6′6″ (610 × 1981 mm)	1 no	1:30	48.60	6	62.00
2′3″ × 6′6″ (686 × 1981 mm)	1 no	1:30	48.60	6	62.00
2′6″ × 6′6″ (762 × 1981 mm)	1 no	1:30	48.60	6	62.00
Interior casement doors pre-glazed with clear or obscure safety glass					
1⅜″ (35 mm) thick door pattern 2XGG					
2′3″ × 6′6″ (686 × 1981 mm)	1 no	1:45	78.00	6	110.00
2′6″ × 6′6″ (762 × 1981 mm)	1 no	1:45	78.00	6	110.00
1⅜″ (35 mm) thick door pattern 10					
2′3″ × 6′6″ (686 × 1981 mm)	1 no	1:45	76.00	6	108.00
2′6″ × 6′6″ (762 × 1981 mm)	1 no	1:45	76.00	6	108.00
1⅜″ (35 mm) thick door pattern 2XG					
2′3″ × 6′6″ (686 × 1981 mm)	1 no	1:45	78.90	6	110.00
2′6″ × 6′6″ (762 × 1981 mm)	1 no	1:45	78.90	6	110.00
1⅜″ (35 mm) thick door pattern 50					
2′3″ × 6′6″ (686 × 1981 mm)	1 no	1:45	89.50	6	125.00
2′6″ × 6′6″ (762 × 1981 mm)	1 no	1:45	89.50	6	125.00

Don't forget, these prices may need adjustment depending on where you live.
Regional adjustments are provided on the inside cover, and further explanation is given in the Preface.

Pine louvred doors

1⅛″ (29 mm) thick doors

1′0″ × 1′6″ (305 × 457 mm)	1 no	1:00	5.50	6	12.00
1′6″ × 1′6″ (457 × 457 mm)	1 no	1:00	7.10	6	14.00
1′6″ × 2′0″ (457 × 610 mm)	1 no	1:00	8.60	6	15.00
2′0″ × 1′0″ (610 × 457 mm)	1 no	1:00	8.70	6	12.00
2′0″ × 2′0″ (610 × 610 mm)	1 no	1:00	10.15	6	15.00
1′6″ × 2′6″ (457 × 762 mm)	1 no	1:00	10.25	6	15.00
1′6″ × 3′0″ (457 × 914 mm)	1 no	1:00	11.25	6	17.00
2′0″ × 3′0″ (610 × 914 mm)	1 no	1:00	15.00	6	22.00
1′6″ × 4′0″ (457 × 1220 mm)	1 no	1:10	15.00	6	23.00
1′6″ × 5′0″ (457 × 1524 mm)	1 no	1:20	19.20	6	28.00
1′0″ × 5′6″ (305 × 1676 mm)	1 no	1:20	15.75	6	25.00
1′6″ × 5′6″ (457 × 1676 mm)	1 no	1:20	21.00	6	30.00
1′0″ × 6′0″ (305 × 1829 mm)	1 no	1:20	17.00	6	26.00
1′6″ × 6′0″ (457 × 1829 mm)	1 no	1:20	23.25	6	35.00
2′0″ × 6′0″ (610 × 1829 mm)	1 no	1:20	27.80	6	40.00
1′6″ × 6′6″ (457 × 1981 mm)	1 no	1:50	23.90	6	38.00
2′0″ × 6′6″ (610 × 1981 mm)	1 no	1:50	29.80	6	45.00
2′6″ × 6′6″ (762 × 1981 mm)	1 no	1:50	36.00	6	55.00

Period doors					
1⅜″ (35 mm) thick Marlborough softwood 6 panel door					
2′0″ × 6′6″ (610 × 1981 mm)	1 no	1:30	128.00	6	155.00
2′3″ × 6′6″ (686 × 1981 mm)	1 no	1:30	128.00	6	155.00
2′6″ × 6′6″ (762 × 1981 mm)	1 no	1:30	128.00	6	155.00
2′9″ × 6′6″ (838 × 1981 mm)	1 no	1:30	128.00	6	155.00
Exterior doors for painting					
1¾″ (44 mm) thick flush door type CF1X					
2′0″ × 6′6″ (610 × 1981 mm)	1 no	1:45	37.75	6	60.00
2′3″ × 6′6″ (686 × 1981 mm)	1 no	1:45	37.75	6	60.00
2′6″ × 6′6″ (762 × 1981 mm)	1 no	1:45	37.75	6	60.00
2′8″ × 6′8″ (813 × 2032 mm)	1 no	1:45	39.30	6	62.00
2′9″ × 6′6″ (838 × 1981 mm)	1 no	1:45	39.30	6	62.00
2′9″ × 6′9″ (838 × 2056 mm)	1 no	1:45	40.50	6	62.00
807 × 2000 mm	1 no	1:45	39.40	6	60.00
826 × 2040 mm	1 no	1:45	40.00	6	60.00
1¾″ (44 mm) thick flush door type CF2X					
2′6″ × 6′6″ (762 × 1981 mm)	1 no	1:45	49.25	6	70.00
2′8″ × 6′8″ (813 × 2032 mm)	1 no	1:45	50.50	6	70.00
2′9″ × 6′6″ (838 × 1981 mm)	1 no	1:45	50.50	6	70.00
1¾″ (44 mm) thick flush door type CF3X					
2′6″ × 6′6″ (762 × 1981 mm)	1 no	1:45	49.25	6	70.00

2′8″ × 6′8″ (813 x 2032 mm)	1 no	1:45	50.50	6	70.00
2′9″ × 6′6″ (838 × 1981 mm)	1 no	1:45	50.50	6	70.00
1¾″ (44 mm) thick flush door type CF4X					
2′6″ × 6′6″ (762 × 1981 mm)	1 no	1:45	49.25	6	70.00
2′8″ × 6′8″ (813 × 2032 mm)	1 no	1:45	50.50	6	70.00
2′9″ × 6′6″ (838 × 1981 mm)	1 no	1:45	50.50	6	70.00
1¾″ (44 mm) thick flush door type CF14X					
2′6″ × 6′6″ (762 × 1981 mm)	1 no	1:45	49.25	6	70.00
2′8″ × 6′8″ (813 × 2032 mm)	1 no	1:45	50.50	6	70.00
2′9″ x 6′6″ (838 × 1981 mm)	1 no	1:45	50.00	6	70.00

Exterior casement and panel doors

1¾″ (44 mm) thick door pattern 2XG with loose beads					
2′6″ × 6′6″ (762 × 1981 mm)	1 no	1:45	54.15	6	75.00
2′8″ × 6′8″ (813 × 2032 mm)	1 no	1:45	56.50	6	75.00
2′9″ × 6′6″ (838 × 1981 mm)	1 no	1:45	56.50	6	75.00
807 × 2000 mm	1 no	1:45	56.50	6	75.00
1¾″ (44 mm) thick door pattern 2XGG with loose beads					
2′6″ × 6′6″ (762 × 1981 mm)	1 no	1:45	50.50	6	70.00
2′8″ × 6′8″ (813 × 2032 mm)	1 no	1:45	52.50	6	72.00
2′9″ × 6′6″ (838 × 1981 mm)	1 no	1:45	52.50	6	72.00
807 × 2000 mm	1 no	1:45	52.50	6	72.00

1¾″ (44 mm) thick door pattern 10 with loose beads					
2′6″ × 6′6″ (762 × 1981 mm)	1 no	1:45	44.10	6	65.00
2′8″ × 6′8″ (813 × 2032 mm)	1 no	1:45	44.10	6	65.00
2′9″ × 6′6″ (838 × 1981 mm)	1 no	1:45	44.10	6	65.00
807 × 2000 mm	1 no	1:45	44.10	6	65.00
1¾″ (44 mm) thick door pattern 50					
2′6″ × 6′6″ (762 × 1981 mm)	1 no	1:45	48.35	6	70.00
2′8″ × 6′8″ (813 × 2032 mm)	1 no	1:45	50.25	6	70.00
2′9″ × 6′6″ (838 × 1981 mm)	1 no	1:45	50.25	6	70.00
807 × 2000 mm	1 no	1:45	50.25	6	70.00
1¾″ (44 mm) thick door pattern SA					
2′6″ × 6′6″ (762 × 1981 mm)	1 no	1:45	67.00	6	90.00
2′8″ × 6′8″ (813 × 2032 mm)	1 no	1:45	69.70	6	90.00
2′9″ × 6′6″ (838 × 1981 mm)	1 no	1:45	69.70	6	90.00
807 × 2000 mm	1 no	1:45	69.70	6	90.00
1¾″ (44 mm) thick door pattern 80					
2′6″ × 6′6″ (762 × 1981 mm)	1 no	1:45	54.50	6	75.00
2′8″ × 6′8″ (813 × 2032 mm)	1 no	1:45	62.30	6	85.00
2′9″ × 6′6″ (838 × 1981 mm)	1 no	1:45	62.30	6	85.00
807 × 2000 mm	1 no	1:45	62.30	6	85.00
1¾″ (44 mm) thick door pattern KXTP					
2′6″ × 6′6″ (762 × 1981 mm)	1 no	1:45	84.70	6	100.00
2′8″ × 6′8″ (813 × 2032 mm)	1 no	1:45	88.20	6	110.00

2′9″ × 6′6″ (838 × 1981 mm)	1 no	1:45	88.20	6	110.00
807 × 2000 mm	1 no	1:45	88.20	6	110.00
1¾″ (44 mm) thick door pattern 2XHG					
2′6″ × 6′6″ (762 × 1981 mm)	1 no	1:45	57.60	6	75.00
2′8″ × 6′8″ (813 × 2032 mm)	1 no	1:45	60.70	6	80.00
2′9″ × 6′6″ (838 × 1981 mm)	1 no	1:45	60.70	6	80.00
807 × 2000 mm	1 no	1:45	60.70	6	80.00
1¾″ (44 mm) thick door pattern FX					
2′6″ × 6′6″ (762 × 1981 mm)	1 no	1:45	90.00	6	115.00
2′8″ × 6′8″ (813 × 2032 mm)	1 no	1:45	93.50	6	120.00
2′9″ × 6′6″ (838 × 1981 mm)	1 no	1:45	93.50	6	120.00
807 × 2000 mm	1 no	1:45	93.50	6	120.00
1¾″ (44 mm) thick door pattern 2XGB					
2′6″ × 6′6″ (762 × 1981 mm)	1 no	1:45	76.50	6	100.00
2′8″ × 6′8″ (813 × 2032 mm)	1 no	1:45	79.50	6	105.00
2′9″ × 6′6″ (838 × 1981 mm)	1 no	1:45	79.50	6	105.00
807 × 2000 mm	1 no	1:45	79.50	6	105.00
1¾″ (44 mm) thick door pattern SF					
2′6″ × 6′6″ (762 × 1981 mm)	1 no	1:45	71.20	6	90.00
2′8″ × 6′8″ (813 × 2032 mm)	1 no	1:45	73.70	6	95.00
2′9″ × 6′6″ (838 × 1981 mm)	1 no	1:45	73.70	6	95.00
807 × 2000 mm	1 no	1:45	73.70	6	95.00

1¾″ (44 mm) thick door pattern SC					
2′6″ × 6′6″ (762 × 1981 mm)	1 no	1:45	79.80	6	105.00
2′8″ × 6′8″ (813 × 2032 mm)	1 no	1:45	83.40	6	110.00
2′9″ × 6′6″ (838 × 1981 mm)	1 no	1:45	83.40	6	110.00
807 × 2000 mm	1 no	1:45	83.40	6	110.00
1¾″ (44 mm) thick door pattern P115					
2′6″ × 6′6″ (762 × 1981 mm)	1 no	1:45	89.00	6	115.00
2′8″ × 6′8″ (813 × 2032 mm)	1 no	1:45	92.60	6	120.00
2′9″ × 6′6″ (838 × 1981 mm)	1 no	1:45	92.60	6	120.00
807 × 2000 mm	1 no	1:45	92.60	6	120.00
1¾″ (44 mm) thick door pattern 2XGGS					
2′6″ × 6′6″ (762 × 1981 mm)	1 no	1:45	58.00	6	80.00
2′8″ × 6′8″ (813 × 2032 mm)	1 no	1:45	60.40	6	85.00
2′9″ × 6′6″ (838 × 1981 mm)	1 no	1:45	60.40	6	85.00
807 × 2000 mm	1 no	1:45	60.40	6	85.00
1¾″ (44 mm) thick door pattern 2XGS					
2′6″ × 6′6″ (762 × 1981 mm)	1 no	1:45	60.00	6	85.00
2′8″ × 6′8″ (813 × 2032 mm)	1 no	1:45	64.30	6	90.00
2′9″ × 6′6″ (838 × 1981 mm)	1 no	1:45	64.30	6	90.00
807 × 2000 mm	1 no	1:45	64.30	6	90.00

1¾″ (44 mm) thick door pattern DX					
2′6″ × 6′6″ (762 × 1981 mm)	1 no	1:45	85.60	6	100.00
2′8″ × 6′8″ (813 × 2032 mm)	1 no	1:45	89.20	6	110.00
2′9″ × 6′6″ (838 × 1981 mm)	1 no	1:45	89.20	6	110.00
807 × 2000 mm	1 no	1:45	89.20	6	110.00
1¾″ (44 mm) thick door pattern 20 with loose beads					
3′0″ × 6′6″ (914 × 1981 mm)	1 pair	3:00	94.00	6	140.00
3′10″ × 6′6″ (1168 × 1981 mm)	1 pair	3:00	94.00	6	140.00
1¾″ (44 mm) thick door pattern 22 with loose beads					
3′0″ × 6′6″ (914 × 1981 mm)	1 pair	3:00	112.00	6	160.00
3′10″ × 6′6″ (1168 × 1981 mm)	1 pair	3:00	112.00	6	160.00
1¾″ (44 mm) thick door pattern 70					
3′0″ × 6′6″ (914 × 1981 mm)	1 pair	3:00	100.70	6	150.00
3′10″ × 6′6″ (1168 × 1981 mm)	1 pair	3:00	100.70	6	150.00
1¾″ (44 mm) thick door pattern 2SA					
3′0″ × 6′6″ (914 × 1981 mm)	1 pair	3:00	147.00	6	210.00
3′10″ × 6′6″ (1168 × 1981 mm)	1 pair	3:00	147.00	6	210.00

Don't forget, these prices may need adjustment depending on where you live.

Regional adjustments are provided on the inside cover, and further explanation is given in the Preface.

Exterior casement doors pre-glazed with clear or obscure safety glass					
1¾″ (44 mm) thick door pattern 2XG					
2′6″ × 6′6″ (762 × 1981 mm)	1 no	2:00	84.80	6	130.00
2′8″ × 6′8″ (813 × 2032 mm)	1 no	2:00	84.80	6	130.00
2′9″ × 6′6″ (838 × 1981 mm)	1 no	2:00	84.80	6	130.00
807 × 2000 mm	1 no	2:00	84.80	6	130.00
1¾″ (44 mm) thick door pattern 2XGG					
2′6″ × 6′6″ (762 × 1981 mm)	1 no	2:00	92.60	6	140.00
2′8″ × 6′8″ (813 × 2032 mm)	1 no	2:00	92.60	6	140.00
2′9″ × 6′6″ (838 x 1981 mm)	1 no	2:00	92.60	6	140.00
807 × 2000 mm	1 no	2:00	92.60	6	140.00
1¾″ (44 mm) thick door pattern 10					
2′6″ × 6′6″ (762 × 1981 mm)	1 no	2:00	83.30	6	130.00
2′8″ × 6′8″ (813 × 2032 mm)	1 no	2:00	83.30	6	130.00
2′9″ × 6′6″ (838 × 1981 mm)	1 no	2:00	83.30	6	130.00
807 × 2000 mm	1 no	2:00	83.30	6	130.00
1¾″ (44 mm) thick door pattern 20					
3′10″ × 6′6″ (1168 × 1981 mm)	1 pair	3:30	148.00	6	210.00
1¾″ (44 mm) thick door pattern 22					
3′10″ × 6′6″ (1168 × 1981 mm)	1 pair	3:30	167.50	6	230.00
Matchboarded doors in redwood					
1¾″ (44 mm) thick ledged and braced door					
2′6″ × 6′6″ (762 × 1981 mm)	1 no	1:45	49.30	6	70.00

2′8″ × 6′8″ (813 × 2032 mm)	1 no	1:45	49.30	6	70.00
2′9″ × 6′6″ (838 × 1981 mm)	1 no	1:45	49.30	6	70.00
726 × 2040 mm	1 no	1:45	49.30	6	70.00
826 × 2040 mm	1 no	1:45	49.30	6	70.00
1¾″ (44 mm) thick framed ledged and braced door					
2′3″ × 6′6″ (686 × 1981 mm)	1 no	1:45	64.70	6	85.00
2′6″ × 6′6″ (762 × 1981 mm)	1 no	1:45	64.70	6	85.00
2′8″ × 6′8″ (813 × 2032 mm)	1 no	1:45	64.70	6	85.00
2′9″ × 6′6″ (838 × 1981 mm)	1 no	1:45	64.70	6	85.00
Garage doors in redwood					
1¾″ (44 mm) thick doors pattern CGG					
7′0″ × 6′6″ (2135 × 1981 mm)	1 pair	8:00	200.00	6	300.00
7′0″ × 7′0″ (2135 × 2135 mm)	1 pair	8:00	200.00	6	300.00
1¾″ (44 mm) thick doors pattern CGP					
7′0″ × 6′6″ (2135 × 1981 mm)	1 pair	8:00	183.00	6	290.00
7′0″ x 7′0″ (2135 × 2135 mm)	1 pair	8:00	183.00	6	290.00

Don't forget, these prices may need adjustment depending on where you live.
Regional adjustments are provided on the inside cover, and further explanation is given in the Preface.

Period doors

These doors can provide a very attractive feature to the front entrance of your house. The prices given apply to each size of door within the range. The sizes available are:

2′9″ × 6′6″ (838 × 1981 mm)
2′8″ × 6′8″ (813 × 2032 mm)
2′6″ × 6′6″ (762 × 1981 mm)
807 × 2000 mm (no imperial size equivalent)

1⅜″ (44 mm) thick door in Brazilian mahogany in sizes					
Portcullis	1 no	2:00	195.00	6	230.00
Gothic half light	1 no	2:00	212.00	6	250.00
6 panel	1 no	2:00	217.00	6	255.00
4 panel	1 no	2:00	217.00	6	255.00
4 panel fanlight	1 no	2:00	247.00	6	285.00
Tudor	1 no	2:00	254.00	6	290.00
Knightsbridge	1 no	2:00	248.00	6	285.00
Half bow	1 no	2:00	232.00	6	265.00
Kentucky	1 no	2:00	222.00	6	260.00
Chelsea	1 no	2:00	187.00	6	220.00
1¾″ (44 mm) thick door in Canadian softwood in sizes					
Carolina	1 no	2:00	140.00	6	175.00
Kentucky	1 no	2:00	130.00	6	165.00
Elizabethan	1 no	2:00	165.00	6	200.00
Gothic half light	1 no	2:00	135.00	6	170.00
Half bow	1 no	2:00	140.00	6	175.00
4 panel	1 no	2:00	145.00	6	180.00
Portcullis	1 no	2:00	105.00	6	140.00
6 panel	1 no	2:00	145.00	6	180.00
Knightsbridge	1 no	2:00	160.00	6	195.00
Chelsea	1 no	2:00	120.00	6	155.00
1¾″ (44 mm) thick door in red meranti in sizes					
Carolina	1 no	2:00	193.00	6	235.00
Kentucky	1 no	2:00	185.00	6	230.00
Elizabethan	1 no	2:00	207.00	6	250.00
Chelsea	1 no	2:00	152.00	6	200.00
6 panel	1 no	2:00	190.00	6	235.00
4 panel	1 no	2:00	190.00	6	250.00

Gothic half light	1 no	2:00	195.00	6	240.00
Portcullis	1 no	2:00	176.00	6	225.00
Knightsbridge	1 no	2:00	228.00	6	270.00
Half bow	1 no	2:00	221.00	6	265.00
2XGGM	1 no	2:00	94.00	6	150.00
2XGM	1 no	2:00	107.00	6	160.00
10M	1 no	2:00	84.00	6	140.00
SAM	1 no	2:00	122.00	6	175.00
22M	1 pair	4:00	184.00	6	330.00
2SAM	1 pair	4:00	210.00	6	350.00

Ironmongery

There is a wide variation in the range and quality of ironmongery you can buy and the following list is based upon average quality products.

The following hours are based upon fixing the ironmongery to softwood and you should add approximately 15% to the figures quoted for fixing to hardwood.

Hinges					
Light steel butts					
2″ (50 mm)	1 pair	0:30	0.40	4	2.50
3″ (75 mm)	1 pair	0:35	0.50	4	2.75
4″ (100 mm)	1 pair	0:40	0.60	4	3.00
Medium steel butts					
3″ (75 mm)	1 pair	0:35	1.30	4	4.40
4″ (100 mm)	1 pair	0:40	1.70	4	5.00
Heavy steel butts					
4″ (100 mm)	1 pair	0:40	2.30	4	6.30
Brass butts with brass pins					
2″ (50 mm)	1 pair	0:30	1.80	4	5.00
3″ (75 mm)	1 pair	0:35	2.40	4	6.50
4″ (100 mm)	1 pair	0:40	5.00	4	9.00
Heavy duty hook and band hinges					
12″ (300 mm)	1 pair	1:80	6.00	4	15.00
18″ (450 mm)	1 pair	2:00	8.50	4	20.00
24″ (600 mm)	1 pair	2:20	13.00	4	25.00

Bolts					
Steel barrel bolts					
4″ (100 mm)	1 nr	0:20	1.40	5	2.50
6″ (150 mm)	1 nr	0:20	1.70	5	3.00
8″ (200 mm)	1 nr	0:25	2.10	5	3.50
12″ (300 mm)	1 nr	0:25	3.15	5	4.50
Brass barrel bolts					
3″ (75 mm)	1 nr	0:20	1.60	5	3.00
4″ (100 mm)	1 nr	0:20	1.90	5	3.30
6″ (150 mm)	1 nr	0:20	2.10	5	3.50
Aluminium barrel bolts					
3″ (75 mm)	1 nr	0:20	1.60	5	3.00
4″ (100 mm)	1 nr	0:20	1.80	5	3.30
6″ (150 mm)	1 nr	0:20	2.00	5	3.40
Locks					
Black japanned rim lock	1 nr	2:00	4.70	5	11.00
Black japanned rim dead lock	1 nr	2:00	6.20	5	14.00
Mortice lock	1 nr	2:00	5.20	5	11.00
Mortice dead lock	1 nr	2:00	6.20	5	12.50
Latches					
Cylinder night latch	1 nr	2:30	11.40	5	18.00
Thumb latch	1 nr	1:00	2.60	5	8.00
Mortice latch	1 nr	2:00	4.00	5	12.00
Rebated mortice latch	1 nr	2:00	4.70	5	14.00
Door furniture					
Aluminium pull handle					
6″ (150 mm)	1 nr	0:30	3.00	5	5.00
9″ (225 mm)	1 nr	0:35	7.20	5	9.00
12″ (300 mm)	1 nr	0:40	9.80	5	13.00
Aluminium lever handle	1 set	1:00	5.30	5	10.00
Aluminium letter plate (hole in door already cut)	1 nr	0:30	5.30	5	9.00
Door viewer	1 nr	1:00	8.00	5	16.00

Windows

One of the most dramatic changes you can make to the appearance of your house that does not involve structural alterations is the fitting of new windows. The information used in this section was supplied by John Carr Joinery Sales Ltd, Watch House Lane, Doncaster, South Yorkshire, DN5 9LR.

Standard windows are manufactured both in metric and imperial sizes and it is likely that if your house is over ten years old you would require windows in imperial dimensions. You can buy windows which are already glazed at the factory in single, double glazing or leaded lights. This option is only available for double glazing if you buy six or more windows but you can buy glass cut to size for all windows in any quantity to fix yourself. The following illustrations of windows have the references shown in John Carr's catalogue. Window HN07V refers to a window with a single top hung opening light, overall size 488 mm wide by 750 mm high. The letters HN and V refer to the style of the window while the figures 07 refer to the height. The purpose of the illustration is to show the style of the window so the reference appears as HN..V and the varying heights will appear in the item descriptions. Only the most popular sizes are given and there are many more standard sizes available.

Hardwood windows in metric sizes					
Red mahogany casement windows with easy clean hinges reference					
HN09V size 488 × 900 mm high	1 no	1:10	76.00	5	100.00
H110C size 630 × 1050 mm high	1 no	1:30	92.00	5	115.00
H112C size 630 × 1200 mm high	1 no	1:30	95.00	5	120.00
H112T size 630 × 1200 mm high	1 no	1:30	130.00	5	170.00
H109V size 630 × 900 mm high	1 no	1:30	84.00	5	110.00

Hardwood windows in metric sizes

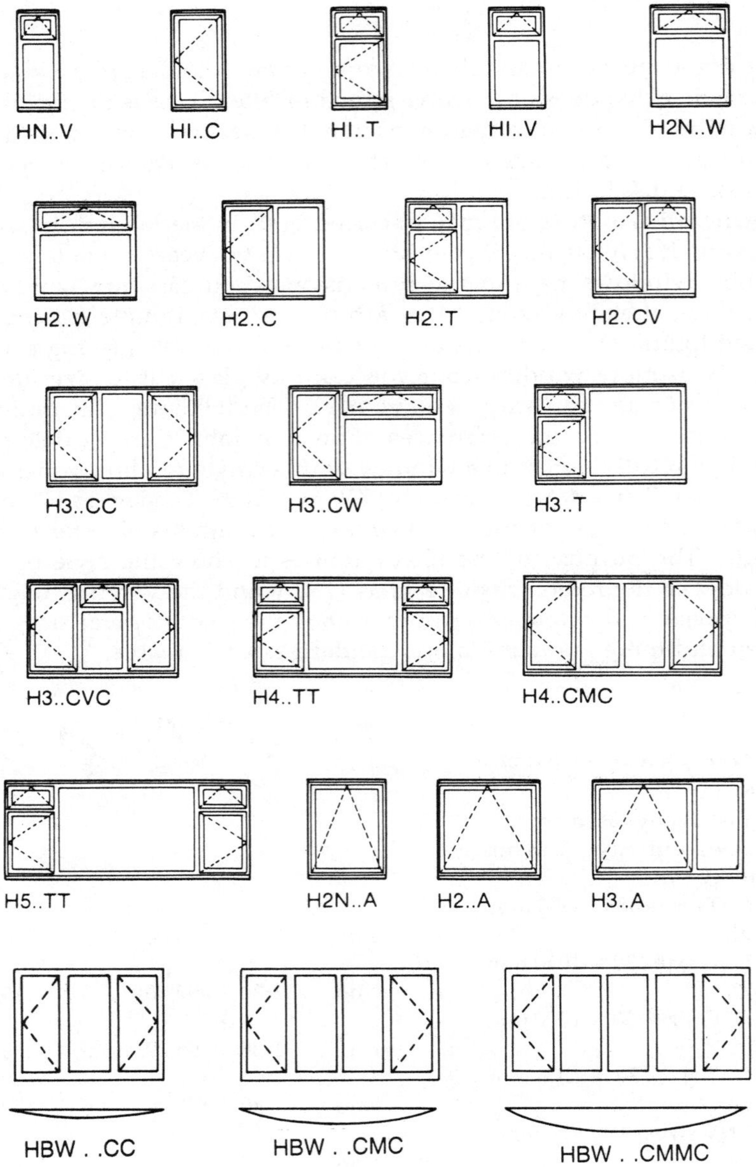
HN..V
HI..C
HI..T
HI..V
H2N..W
H2..W
H2..C
H2..T
H2..CV
H3..CC
H3..CW
H3..T
H3..CVC
H4..TT
H4..CMC
H5..TT
H2N..A
H2..A
H3..A
HBW . .CC
HBW . .CMC
HBW . .CMMC

Softwood windows in imperial sizes

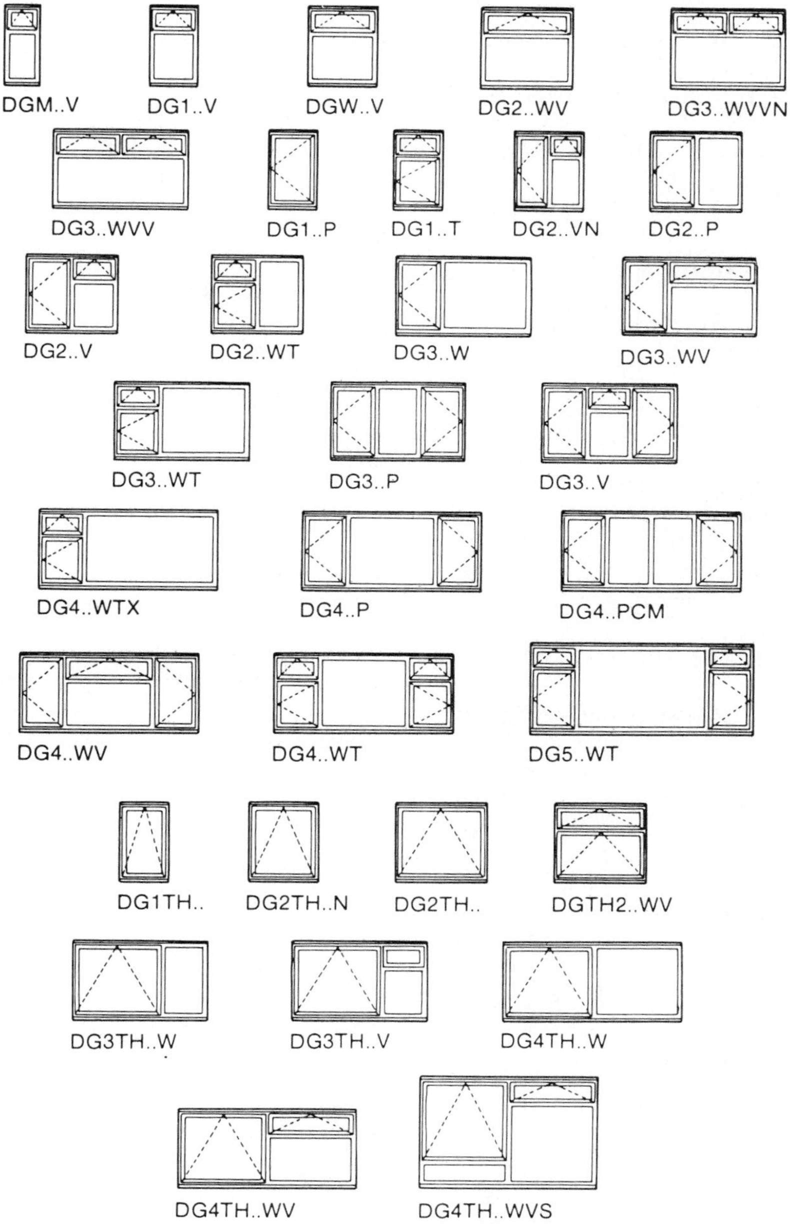
DGM..V
DG1..V
DGW..V
DG2..WV
DG3..WVVN
DG3..WVV
DG1..P
DG1..T
DG2..VN
DG2..P
DG2..V
DG2..WT
DG3..W
DG3..WV
DG3..WT
DG3..P
DG3..V
DG4..WTX
DG4..P
DG4..PCM
DG4..WV
DG4..WT
DG5..WT
DG1TH..
DG2TH..N
DG2TH..
DGTH2..WV
DG3TH..W
DG3TH..V
DG4TH..W
DG4TH..WV
DG4TH..WVS

H110V size 630 × 1050 mm high	1 no	1:30	87.00	5	113.00
H112V size 630 × 1200 mm high	1 no	1:30	88.00	5	113.00
H2N09W size 915 × 900 mm high	1 no	1:45	98.00	5	125.00
H2N10W size 915 × 1050 mm high	1 no	1:45	100.00	5	125.00
H2N12W size 915 × 1200 mm high	1 no	1:45	102.00	5	130.00
H210W size 1200 × 1050 mm high	1 no	2:30	118.00	5	150.00
H212W size 1200 × 1200 mm high	1 no	2:30	120.00	5	150.00
H209C size 1200 × 900 mm high	1 no	2:30	118.00	5	150.00
H210C size 1200 × 1050 mm high	1 no	2:30	122.00	5	155.00
H212C size 1200 × 1200 mm high	1 no	2:30	127.00	5	160.00
H213C size 1200 × 1350 mm high	1 no	2:30	135.00	5	175.00
H210T size 1200 × 1050 mm high	1 no	2:30	153.00	5	190.00
H210CV size 1200 × 1050 mm high	1 no	2:30	155.00	5	195.00
H212CV size 1200 × 1200 mm high	1 no	2:30	160.00	5	200.00
H310CC size 1770 × 1050 mm high	1 no	3:00	196.00	5	250.00
H312CC size 1770 × 1200 mm high	1 no	3:00	207.00	5	260.00
H313CC size 1770 × 1350 mm high	1 no	3:00	218.00	5	275.00
H310CW size 1770 × 1050 mm high	1 no	3:00	185.00	5	240.00
H312CW size 1770 × 1200 mm high	1 no	3:00	190.00	5	245.00
H310T size 1770 × 1050 mm high	1 no	3:00	175.00	5	230.00
H312T size 1770 × 1200 mm high	1 no	3:00	180.00	5	235.00

H310CVC size 1770 × 1050 mm high	1 no	3:00	225.00	5	280.00
H312CVC size 1770 × 1200 mm high	1 no	3:00	232.00	5	290.00
H313CVC size 1770 × 1350 mm high	1 no	3:00	240.00	5	300.00
H410TT size 2339 × 1050 mm high	1 no	3:30	282.00	5	350.00
H412TT size 2339 × 1200 mm high	1 no	3:30	290.00	5	375.00
H413TT size 2339 × 1350 mm high	1 no	3:30	295.00	5	380.00
H410CMC size 2339 × 1050 mm high	1 no	3:30	240.00	5	300.00
H412CMC size 2339 × 1200 mm high	1 no	3:30	247.00	5	305.00
H413CMC size 2339 × 1350 mm high	1 no	3:30	258.00	5	330.00
H513TT size 2908 × 1350 mm high	1 no	4:00	346.00	5	450.00
Red mahogany bow windows with easy clean hinges reference					
HBW13CC size 1781 × 1350 mm	1 no	3:00	385.00	5	480.00
HBW13CMC size 2340 × 1350 mm	1 no	3:30	468.00	5	550.00
HBW13CMMC size 2888 × 1350 mm	1 no	4:00	555.00	5	650.00

Don't forget, these prices may need adjustment depending on where you live.

Regional adjustments are provided on the inside cover, and further explanation is given in the Preface.

Softwood windows

The following windows are manufactured in imperial sizes and should be ideal for replacement if your existing windows are more than approximately ten years old. They are manufactured in Scandinavian redwood and stained to give a hardwood appearance and the prices include loose stained glazing beads. Alternatively the windows can be supplied factory-primed for painting at the same price.

Softwood windows with butt hinges in imperial sizes reference					
N26V size 1′5¼″ × 2′6¼″	1 no	1:10	35.00	5	50.00
N36V size 1′5¼″ × 3′6¼″	1 no	1:30	38.00	5	55.00
130V size 2′1¼″ × 3′0¼″	1 no	1:30	40.00	5	60.00
140V size 2′1¼″ × 4′0¼″	1 no	1:30	43.00	5	65.00
W36V size 3′0¼″ × 3′6¼″	1 no	1:45	50.00	5	70.00
W46V size 3′0¼″ × 4′6¼″	1 no	1:45	52.00	5	75.00
240WV size 4′0¼″ × 4′0¼″	1 no	2:30	62.00	5	85.00
250WV size 4′0¼″ × 5′0¼″	1 no	2:30	66.00	5	90.00
340WVYN size 5′0¼″ × 4′0¼″	1 no	2:30	75.00	5	100.00
346WVV size 5′11½″ × 4′6¼″	1 no	3:00	82.00	5	110.00
126P size 2′11¼″ × 2′6¼″	1 no	1:30	42.00	5	60.00
136P size 2′11¼″ × 3′6¼″	1 no	1:45	44.00	5	65.00
140T size 2′1¼″ × 4′0¼″	1 no	1:30	63.00	5	85.00
230VN size 3′0¼″ × 3′0¼″	1 no	1:45	73.00	5	95.00
236P size 4′0¼″ × 3′6¼″	1 no	2:00	58.00	5	80.00
246P size 4′0¼″ × 4′6¼″	1 no	2:30	64.00	5	85.00
236V size 4′0¼″ × 3′6¼″	1 no	2:00	73.00	5	100.00
246V size 4′0¼″ × 4′6¼″	1 no	2:30	78.00	5	105.00
230WT size 4′0¼″ × 3′0¼″	1 no	2:00	70.00	5	90.00
240WT size 4′0¼″ × 4′0¼″	1 no	2:30	75.00	5	100.00
336W size 5′11¼″ × 3′6¼″	1 no	3:00	70.00	5	95.00
330WV size 5′11¼″ × 3′0¼″	1 no	3:00	90.00	5	115.00
346WV size 5′11¼″ × 4′6¼″	1 no	3:00	95.00	5	120.00
340WT size 5′11¼″ × 4′0¼″	1 no	3:00	86.00	5	110.00
330P size 5′11¼″ × 3′0¼″	1 no	3:00	88.00	5	115.00
346P size 5′11¼″ × 4′6¼″	1 no	3:30	100.00	5	130.00
330V size 5′11¼″ × 3′0¼″	1 no	3:00	98.00	5	120.00
436WTX size 7′10¼″ × 3′6¼″	1 no	3:30	90.00	5	115.00
440P size 7′10¼″ × 4′0¼″	1 no	4:00	104.00	5	140.00
446PCM size 7′10¼″ × 4′6¼″	1 no	4:30	115.00	5	165.00
440WV size 7′10¼″ × 4′0¼″	1 no	4:00	125.00	5	170.00

440WT size 7′10¼″ × 4′0¼″	1 no	4:00	132.00	5	180.00
546WT size 9′9¼″ × 4′6¼″	1 no	5:00	150.00	5	220.00
1TH26 size 2′1¼″ × 2′6¼″	1 no	1:30	37.00	5	55.00
1TH36 size 2′1¼″ × 3′6¼″	1 no	1:30	42.00	5	60.00
2TH30H size 3′0¼″ × 3′0¼″	1 no	1:45	53.00	5	70.00
2TH40H size 3′0¼″ × 4′0¼″	1 no	1:45	59.00	5	80.00
2TH20H size 4′0¼″ × 2′0¼″	1 no	1:45	55.00	5	75.00
2TH40 size 4′0¼″ × 4′0¼″	1 no	2:30	63.00	5	85.00
TH236WV size 4′0¼″ × 3′6¼″	1 no	2:00	88.00	5	120.00
3TH26W size 5′11¼″ × 2′6¼″	1 no	2:30	71.00	5	110.00
3TH36W size 5′11¼″ × 3′6¼″	1 no	2:30	75.00	5	115.00
3TH40V size 5′11¼″ × 4′0¼″	1 no	3:00	97.00	5	120.00
4TH26W size 7′10¼″ × 2′6¼″	1 no	2:30	83.00	5	105.00
4TH36W size 7′10¼″ × 3′6¼″	1 no	3:00	87.00	5	115.00
4TH40WV size 7′10¼″ × 4′0¼″	1 no	3:30	118.00	5	150.00
4TH50WVS size 7′10¼″ × 5′0¼″	1 no	5:00	121.00	5	190.00

Glazing

The cost of buying glass cut to size from the window supplier is set out below for some of the above windows. These costs are for the supply of the glass only and not the fixing.

	Plain double glazing	Obscure double glazing	Leaded light double glazing
Hardwood windows			
HN110C size 630 × 1050 mm	25.00	28.00	60.00
H112T size 630 × 1200 mm	36.00	42.00	88.00
H109V size 630 × 900 mm	32.00	37.00	78.00
H2N10W size 915 × 1050 mm	40.00	46.00	98.00
H212W size 1200 × 1200 mm	46.00	53.00	112.00
H213C size 1200 × 1350 mm	65.00	75.00	160.00
H310CC size 1770 × 1050 mm	78.00	90.00	190.00
H312CW size 1770 × 1200 mm	82.00	94.00	200.00
H312CVC size 1770 × 1200 mm	95.00	109.00	230.00
H412TT size 2339 × 1200 mm	122.00	140.00	300.00
H413CMC size 2339 x×1350 mm	130.00	150.00	318.00
H515TT size 2908 × 1500 mm	204.00	235.00	500.00

	Plain double glazing	Obscure double glazing	Leaded light double glazing
Softwood windows			
N26V size 1′5¼″ × 2′6¼″	28.00	32.00	60.00
N36V size 1′5¼″ × 3′6¼″	33.00	38.00	69.00
130V size 2′1¼″ × 3′0¼″	34.00	39.00	83.00
140V size 2′1¼″ × 4′0¼″	41.00	47.00	101.00
W36V size 3′0¼″ × 3′6¼″	43.00	50.00	105.00
W46V size 3′4″ × 4′6¼″	54.00	62.00	130.00
240WV size 4′0¼″ × 4′0¼″	58.00	67.00	141.00
250WV size 4′0¼″ × 5′0¼″	73.00	84.00	177.00
340WVYN size 5′0¼″ × 4′0¼″	74.00	85.00	170.00
346WVV size 5′11½″ × 4′6¼″	91.00	105.00	216.00
126P size 2′11¼″ × 2′6¼″	20.00	23.00	50.00
136P size 2′11¼″ × 3′6¼″	26.00	30.00	64.00
140T size 2′1¼″ × 4′0¼″	38.00	44.00	93.00
230VN size 3′0¼″ × 3′0¼″	46.00	53.00	113.00
236P size 4′0¼″ × 3′6¼″	57.00	66.00	138.00
246P size 4′0¼″ × 4′6¼″	70.00	81.00	157.00
236V size 4′0¼″ × 3′6¼″	62.00	71.00	150.00
246V size 4′0¼″ × 4′6¼″	78.00	90.00	194.00
230WT size 4′0¼″ × 3′0¼″	58.00	67.00	132.00
240WT size 4′0¼″ × 4′0¼″	71.00	82.00	171.00
336W size 5′11¼″ × 3′6¼″	76.00	87.00	181.00
330WV size 5′11¼″ × 3′0¼″	73.00	84.00	177.00
346WV size 5′11¼″ × 4′6¼″	100.00	115.00	230.00
340WT size 5′11¼″ × 4′0¼″	94.00	108.00	225.00
330P size 5′11¼″ × 3′0¼″	80.00	92.00	191.00
346P size 5′11¼″ × 4′6¼″	103.00	118.00	226.00
330V glazing	85.00	98.00	205.00
436WTX glazing	90.00	104.00	229.00
440P glazing	116.00	133.00	277.00
446PCM glazing	140.00	161.00	315.00
440WV glazing	118.00	136.00	284.00
440WT glazing	132.00	152.00	316.00
546WT glazing	164.00	189.00	392.00
1TH26 glazing	20.00	23.00	50.00
1TH36 glazing	26.00	30.00	64.00
2TH30N glazing	29.00	33.00	70.00
2TH40N glazing	38.00	44.00	94.00
2TH20 glazing	28.00	32.00	67.00
2TH40 glazing	48.00	55.00	118.00
TH236WV glazing	48.00	55.00	119.00

	Plain double glazing	Obscure double glazing	Leaded light double glazing
3TH26W glazing	55.00	63.00	132.00
3TH36W glazing	77.00	89.00	187.00
3TH40V glazing	90.00	106.00	217.00
4TH26W glazing	71.00	82.00	169.00
4TH36W glazing	95.00	109.00	231.00
4TH40WV glazing	106.00	122.00	257.00
4TH50WVS glazing	145.00	167.00	354.00

For information on single glazing see p.119.

Don't forget, these prices may need adjustment depending on where you live.
Regional adjustments are provided on the inside cover, and further explanation is given in the Preface.

Kitchens

The variation in quality of kitchen fittings varies from adequate to first class, with the equivalent difference in cost. In this section the cost of materials and the cost of a contractor carrying out the work is expressed as a range. Although it is unlikely that you could buy any satisfactory products much below the bottom of the range, there is hardly any limit to the amount you pay above the top figure quoted. For example a hand made imported Italian kitchen could be an extremely expensive item indeed. It is intended that the following figures reflect the range of products you can see in your local DIY supermarket.

Kitchen fittings these days are sold in two ways. First in the traditional product which is assembled and ready to fit in your kitchen. The second are the 'flat pack' or 'self assembly' units which are sold in kit form for you to make up and fit yourself. The latter is obviously much cheaper to buy but requires more of your time for the assembly and fitting. All the sizes are given in metric and the prices include VAT.

Ready assembled units					
Floor cupboards 870 mm high × 570 mm deep					
300 mm wide	1 no	1:00	60–120	5	75–140
500 mm wide	1 no	1:00	40–135	5	55–160
600 mm wide	1 no	1:00	70–145	5	85–170
1000 mm wide corner unit	1 no	1:20	60–160	5	75–190
1000 mm wide sink or hob unit	1 no	1:20	40–190	5	55–220
Floor cupboards 870 mm high × 570 mm deep with top drawers					
300 mm wide	1 no	1:00	90–170	5	110–200
500 mm wide	1 no	1:00	95–170	5	115–200
600 mm wide	1 no	1:00	100–180	5	120–210
1000 mm wide	1 no	1:20	130–270	5	155–310
1000 mm wide corner unit	1 no	1:20	115–190	5	150–230
1000 mm wide sink unit	1 no	1:20	120–250	5	140–290
1000 mm wide hob unit	1 no	1:20	110–240	5	130–280

Larder units 570 mm deep × 500 mm wide					
2060 mm high	1 no	1:30	200–300	5	230–340
2351 mm high	1 no	1:30	300–400	5	340–450
Oven housing units 570 mm deep × 600 mm wide					
2060 mm high	1 no	1:30	160–340	5	200–400
2351 mm high	1 no	1:30	240–470	5	285–550
Wall units 710 mm high × 279 mm deep					
300 mm wide	1 no	1:00	60–110	5	75–130
500 mm wide	1 no	1:00	30–120	5	45–140
600 mm wide	1 no	1:00	70–140	5	85–165
1000 mm wide	1 no	1:20	40–180	5	55–210
600 mm wide corner unit	1 no	1:20	40–130	5	55–155
500 mm wide with glazed door	1 no	1:00	130–150	5	155–175
1000 mm wide with two glazed doors	1 no	1:20	200–230	5	230–265
Wall units 1001 mm high × 279 mm deep					
300 mm wide	1 no	1:00	110–150	5	130–175
500 mm wide	1 no	1:00	130–170	5	155–200
1000 mm wide	1 no	1:20	180–240	5	285–210
600 mm wide corner unit	1 no	1:20	160–200	5	200–230
'Flat pack' or 'Self Assembly' units (from the 'Banquet' range from B & Q)					
'Highline' base units 870 mm high × 570 mm deep, width					
300 mm	1 no	2:00	40–70	5	55–90
400 mm	1 no	2:00	50–75	5	65–95
500 mm	1 no	2:00	20–80	5	35–100
600 mm	1 no	2:00	45–85	5	60–105
1000 mm sink/hob unit	1 no	2:30	25–120	5	40–150
900 × 900 mm corner unit	1 no	2:30	35–90	5	50–110
600 mm pan drawer unit	1 no	2:00	90–150	5	110–190
Built under oven housing	1 no	2:00	50–65	5	65–85

'Drawerline' base units 870 mm high × 570 mm deep, width					
300 mm	1 no	2:00	50–100	5	65–125
400 mm	1 no	2:00	65–100	5	85–125
500 mm	1 no	2:00	35–105	5	50–130
600 mm	1 no	2:00	55–110	5	70–135
600 mm sink/hob unit	1 no	2:30	55–105	5	70–130
900 × 900 mm corner unit	1 no	2:30	100–170	5	125–210
1000 mm corner unit	1 no	2:30	50–110	5	65–135
1000 mm hob unit	1 no	2:30	60–140	5	80–180
1000 mm sink unit	1 no	2:30	50–145	5	65–185
1000 mm unit	1 no	2:30	60–160	5	80–200
Wall units 712 mm high × 279 mm deep, width					
300 mm	1 no	2:00	40–70	5	55–90
400 mm	1 no	2:00	50–75	5	65–95
500 mm	1 no	2:00	25–80	5	40–100
600 mm	1 no	2:00	45–85	5	60–105
1000 mm	1 no	2:00	30–120	5	45–150
600 mm corner unit	1 no	2:30	50–90	5	65–110
500 mm unit with glass	1 no	2:30	100.00	5	125.00
500 mm peninsula unit	1 no	2:30	130.00	5	155.00
500 mm deeper unit	1 no	2:30	130.00	5	155.00
Worktops					
30 mm thick × 600 mm wide, length					
1000 mm	1 no	0:30	12.00	5	20.00
2000 mm	1 no	0:40	20.00	5	35.00
3000 mm	1 no	0:50	25.00	5	40.00
1625 × 900 mm breakfast bar	1 no	0:50	60.00	5	80.00
40 mm thick × 600 mm wide, wood effect edging, length					
1500 mm	1 no	0:40	25.00	5	40.00
3000 mm	1 no	0.50	40.00	5	55.00
2125 × 900 mm breakfast bar	1 no	0:50	80.00	5	100.00
40 mm thick × 600 m wide with PVC edging, length					
1500 mm	1 no	0:40	40.00	5	55.00
3000 mm	1 no	0:50	65.00	5	85.00
2125 × 900 mm breakfast bar	1 no	0:50	140.00	5	170.00

40 mm thick × 600 mm wide unedged, length					
1500 mm	1 no	0:40	30.00	5	45.00
3000 mm	1 no	0:50	50.00	5	65.00
2125 × 900 breakfast bar	1 no	0:50	115.00	5	150.00
Sinks and taps					
Stainless steel inset single bowl, single drainer size 940 × 485 mm	1 no	1:00	35.00	5	60.00
Stainless steel inset single bowl, double drainer size 1395 × 485 mm	1 no	1:00	70.00	5	100.00
Stainless steel inset luxury 1½ bowl size 965 × 510 mm including accessories	1 no	1:00	100.00	5	135.00
Stainless steel inset luxury 1¾ bowl size 1110 × 510 mm including accessories	1 no	1:00	130.00	5	170.00
Stainless steel inset luxury 2½ bowl size 965 × 510 mm including accessories	1 no	1:00	130.00	5	170.00
'Monobloc' 8″ mixer taps	1 no	1:30	50.00	5	80.00
'Ceramico' ¼ twin 'Munobloc' mixer taps	1 no	1:30	53.00	5	85.00
Sundries					
Towel rail	1 no	0:10	3.00	5	8.00
Single storage racks	1 no	0:20	3.00	5	8.00
Double storage racks	1 no	0:25	4.00	5	10.00
4 tier spice rack	1 no	0:20	4.00	5	10.00
Cutlery tray 1.5 mm thick	1 no	0:10	4.00	5	10.00
Cutlery tray 3 mm thick	1 no	0:10	6.00	5	12.00
Shallow sliding basket 100 mm deep	1 no	0:15	7.00	5	12.00
Deep sliding basket 200 mm deep	1 no	0:20	8.00	5	15.00
Waste bin	1 no	0:20	11.00	5	20.00
Copper canopy hood	1 no	0:40	50.00	5	80.00
Pull out table	1 no	5:00	70.00	5	135.00
Pull out ironing board	1 no	5:00	80.00	5	110.00

If the cost of a new complete kitchen refit is too expensive for you, there is another way in which you can achieve almost the same effect without spending so much. Woodfit Ltd of Chorley Lancs specialise in supplying kitchen cupboard doors and drawer fronts together with a wide range of associated ironmongery.

You can change your kitchen from white melamine to dark oak therefore without disturbing the base units. The following information gives a brief selection of the choices available. For full details send 95p for a catalogue to Woodfit Ltd, Kem Mill, Whittle-le-Woods, Chorley, Lancashire, PR6 7EA. Here are the costs of some of their products and associated hours.

Solid medium oak fronts					
Drawer fronts 140 mm high					
495 mm wide	1 no	0:30	12.37	6	17.00
595 mm wide	1 no	0:30	13.98	6	18.00
Doors 570 mm high					
495 mm wide	1 no	1:00	39.24	6	55.00
595 mm wide	1 no	1:00	43.33	6	60.00
Doors 900 mm high					
495 mm wide	1 no	1:20	60.19	6	75.00
595 mm wide	1 no	1:20	68.19	6	85.00
Solid antique pine fronts					
Drawer fronts 140 mm high					
495 mm wide	1 no	0:30	11.76	6	17.00
595 mm wide	1 no	0:30	13.10	6	18.00
Doors 570 mm high					
495 mm wide	1 no	1:00	36.77	6	50.00
595 mm wide	1 no	1:00	40.59	6	55.00
Doors 900 mm high					
495 mm wide	1 no	1:20	56.86	6	75.00
595 mm wide	1 no	1:20	65.25	6	85.00

Don't forget, these prices may need adjustment depending on where you live.
Regional adjustments are provided on the inside cover, and further explanation is given in the Preface.

Solid maple fronts					
Drawer fronts 140 mm high					
495 mm wide	1 no	0:30	16.22	6	25.00
595 mm wide	1 no	0:30	18.28	6	28.00
Doors 570 mm high					
495 mm wide	1 no	1:00	56.04	6	75.00
595 mm wide	1 no	1:00	64.43	6	85.00
Doors 900 mm high					
495 mm wide	1 no	1:20	81.94	6	105.00
595 mm wide	1 no	1:20	94.87	6	125.00
'Softform' fronts with medium oak trim					
Drawer fronts 140 mm high					
495 mm wide	1 no	0:30	10.93	6	17.00
595 mm wide	1 no	0:30	11.82	6	18.00
Doors 570 mm high					
495 mm wide	1 no	1:00	18.45	6	30.00
595 mm wide	1 no	1:00	20.52	6	35.00
Doors 900 mm high					
495 mm wide	1 no	1:20	25.45	6	40.00
595 mm wide	1 no	1:20	28.39	6	45.00
'Softform' fronts with mahogany trim					
Drawer fronts 140 mm high					
495 mm wide	1 no	0:30	10.93	6	17.00
595 mm wide	1 no	0:30	11.82	6	18.00
Doors 570 mm high					
495 mm wide	1 no	1:00	18.45	6	30.00
595 mm wide	1 no	1:00	20.52	6	35.00
Doors 900 mm high					
495 mm wide	1 no	1:20	25.48	6	40.00
595 mm wide	1 no	1:20	28.39	6	45.00
'Softform' fronts with cherry trim					
Drawer fronts 140 mm high					
495 mm wide	1 no	0:30	11.23	6	18.00
595 mm wide	1 no	0:30	12.13	6	20.00

Doors 570 mm high					
495 mm wide	1 no	1:00	19.98	6	35.00
595 mm wide	1 no	1:00	22.24	6	40.00
Doors 900 mm high					
495 mm wide	1 no	1:20	27.95	6	45.00
595 mm wide	1 no	1:20	31.17	6	50.00
Textured laminated fronts with maple trim					
Drawer fronts 140 mm high					
495 mm wide	1 no	0:30	8.60	6	14.00
595 mm wide	1 no	0:30	9.57	6	15.00
Doors 570 mm high					
495 mm wide	1 no	1:00	15.11	6	25.00
595 mm wide	1 no	1:00	16.97	6	27.00
Doors 900 mm high					
495 mm wide	1 no	1:20	19.86	6	35.00
595 mm wide	1 no	1:20	22.56	6	40.00
Textured laminated fronts with oak trim					
Drawer fronts 140 mm high					
495 mm wide	1 no	0:30	8.60	6	14.00
595 mm wide	1 no	0:30	9.57	6	15.00
Doors 570 mm high					
495 mm wide	1 no	1:00	15.11	6	25.00
595 mm wide	1 no	1:00	16.97	6	27.00
Doors 900 mm high					
495 mm wide	1 no	1:20	19.86	6	35.00
595 mm wide	1 no	1:20	22.56	6	40.00

Woodfit Ltd also stock a large range of hinges, handles etc. and you can order by post.

Don't forget, these prices may need adjustment depending on where you live.
Regional adjustments are provided on the inside cover, and further explanation is given in the Preface.

Wall, floor and ceiling finishes

Applying the finishings to a room is probably the most satisfying of all DIY jobs but because the work that you do will be on permanent view, it also requires the greatest care and skill. Anyone who has not tried plastering before may be surprised to learn that it is one of the hardest skills to master. If you intend to plaster for the first time you would be well advised not to start on the fireplace wall in the lounge which will be facing you every day of your life!

Laying floor and wall tiles can also be more difficult than it seems but patience and care can usually produce an acceptable result.

Alteration work					
Hack off or take up					
wall plaster	1 sq yd	1:00	–	3	3.00
	(1 sq m)	(1:05)			(3.30)
lath and plaster ceiling	1 sq yd	1:00	–	3	3.00
	(1 sq m)	(1:05)			(3.30)
ceramic tiles and backing	1 sq yd	1:10	–	3	3.20
	(1 sq m)	(1:20)			(3.50)
quarry tiles and backing	1 sq yd	1:20	–	3	3.30
	(1 sq m)	(1:30)			(3.60)
vinyl tiles and backing	1 sq yd	1:10	–	3	3.20
	(1 sq m)	(1:20)			(3.50)
woodblock flooring	1 sq yd	0:30	–	3	1.50
	(1 sq m)	(0:35)			(1.65)
plasterboard and skim	1 sq yd	0:30	–	3	1.50
	(1 sq m)	(0:35)			(1.65)
suspended ceiling	1 sq yd	0:25	–	3	1.30
	(1 sq m)	(0:30)			(1.40)
Floor screeds					
Cement and sand screed laid on concrete and trowelled smooth					
1″ thick	1 sq yd	0:40	1.45	7	4.50
(25 mm)	(1 sq m)	(0:45)	(1.60)		(5.00)
1½″ thick	1 sq yd	0:50	2.20	7	5.50
(38 mm)	(1 sq m)	(0:55)	(2.40)		(6.00)
2″ thick	1 sq yd	1:00	2.90	7	7.50
(50 mm)	(1 sq m)	(1:05)	(3.20)		(8.25)

Plastering					
One coat plaster ¼″ (6 mm) thick to plasterboard					
walls	1 sq yd	0:50	0.90	8	4.80
	(1 sq m)	(0:55)	(1.00)		(5.30)
ceilings	1 sq yd	1:00	0.90	8	5.60
	(1 sq m)	(1:05)	(1.00)		(6.10)
One coat browning undercoat and one coat finishing plaster total thickness ½″ (13 mm)					
brick walls	1 sq yd	1:00	2.00	8	7.00
	(1 sq m)	(1:05)	(2.20)		(7.70)
One coat bonding plaster and one coat finishing plaster total thickness ¾″ (18 mm)					
plasterboard ceilings	1 sq yd	1:10	2.50	8	7.50
	(1 sq m)	(1:20)	(2.75)		(8.25)
Floor tiling					
PVC floor tiles fixed with adhesive to prepared floor screed					
2 mm thick	1 sq yd	0:45	7.00	6	12.00
	(1 sq m)	(0:50)	(7.70)		(13.20)
3.2 mm thick	1 sq yd	0:45	9.00	6	14.00
	(1 sq m)	(0:50)	(9.90)		(15.40)
Woodblock flooring 1″ (25 mm) thick, tongued and grooved, laid to a herringbone pattern, fixing with adhesive and sanding					
Iroko	1 sq yd	1:30	22.25	7	32.00
	(1 sq m)	(1:45)	(26.50)		(36.00)
Merbau	1 sq yd	1:30	22.40	7	32.25
	(1 sq m)	(1:45)	(26.80)		(36.50)
European oak	1 sq yd	1:30	26.50	7	38.00
	(1 sq m)	(1:45)	(31.80)		(42.00)
American oak	1 sq yd	1:30	31.00	7	43.00
	(1 sq m)	(1:45)	(37.00)		(48.00)
Sapele	1 sq yd	1:30	20.00	7	34.00
	(1 sq m)	(1:45)	(23.75)		(38.00)
Mahogany	1 sq yd	1:30	22.00	7	33.00
	(1 sq m)	(1:45)	(26.25)		(36.00)

Maple	1 sq yd	1:30	18.25	7	31.00
	(1 sq m)	(1:45)	(21.75)		(34.00)
Terrazzo tile paving 1″ (25 mm) thick bedded on screed, joints pointed in white cement	1 sq yd	1:45	21.00	7	33.00
	(1 sq m)	(1:55)	(23.00)		(36.00)
Red quarry tiles laid on screed					
½″ (12 mm) thick	1 sq yd	1:30	14.00	7	22.00
	(1 sq m)	(1:40)	(16.00)		(24.00)
1″ (25 mm) thick	1 sq yd	1:40	20.00	7	28.00
	(1 sq m)	(1:50)	(22.00)		(31.00)
Glazed ceramic tiles size 150 × 150 × 9 mm thick on screed					
grey steel	1 sq yd	1:30	16.00	7	25.00
	(1 sq m)	(1:40)	(17.60)		(27.50)
Stone, granite, rock-face or russet blend					
black	1 sq yd	1:30	13.50	7	23.00
	(1 sq m)	(1:40)	(14.00)		(25.30)
red	1 sq yd	1:30	11.00	7	21.00
	(1 sq m)	(1:40)	(12.00)		(23.10)

Wall tiling

Glazed ceramic wall tiles size 108 × 108 × 4 mm fixed to walls with adhesive and pointed in white cement grout					
white	1 sq yd	2:30	10.20	6	24.00
	(1 sq m)	(2:45)	(11.25)		(26.50)
coloured	1 sq yd	2:30	12.00	6	26.00
	(1 sq m)	(2:45)	(13.25)		(28.50)
Glazed ceramic wall tiles size 152 × 152 × 5.5 mm fixed to walls with adhesive and pointed in white cement grout					
white	1 sq yd	2:00	11.00	6	23.50
	(1 sq m)	(2:10)	(12.20)		(26.00)
coloured	1 sq yd	2:00	12.75	6	23.00
	(1 sq m)	(2:10)	(14.00)		(25.50)

Dry linings					
Insulated plasterboard 9.5 mm thick with taped edges fixed to softwood with galvanised nails, joints taped and filled					
walls	1 sq yd (1 sq m)	1:10 (1:20)	3.75 (4.20)	6	9.80 (10.75)
ceilings	1 sq yd (1 sq m)	1:20 (1:30)	3.75 (4.20)	6	10.50 (11.50)
Paramount dry partition including softwood battens at joints base and head, with all joints taped and filled					
50 mm thick	1 sq yd (1 sq m)	1:30 (1:40)	15.50 (17.00)	6	25.00 (27.50)
63 mm thick	1 sq yd (1 sq m)	1:45 (2:00)	17.50 (19.25)	6	30.00 (33.00)

Rendering and pebble dashing

Applying render (usually a mixture of cement and sand) is an effective method of completely changing the external appearance of your house. It is quite difficult for a DIY enthusiast to produce an overall uniform effect but it can be achieved. Note that scaffolding or tower hire costs are not included here.

Render brick wall in cement and sand in one coat ½″ (12 mm) thick	1 sq yd (1 sq m)	0:50 (1:00)	1.10 (1.30)	7	4.80 (5.75)
Render brick wall with cement and sand in two coats ¾″ (18 mm) thick	1 sq yd (1 sq m)	1:20 (1:35)	1.50 (1.80)	7	6.40 (7.60)
Add to the above prices for the following					
integral waterproof	1 sq yd (1 sq m)	0:05 (0:06)	0.25 (0.28)	3	1.00 (1.10)
rough cast face	1 sq yd (1 sq m)	0:30 (0:35	– –	6	2.80 (3.00)

pebble dash finish	1 sq yd	0:30	0.30	6	3.20
	(1 sq m)	(0:35)	(0.35)		(3.50)
priming and bonding coat	1 sq yd	0:10	0.80	3	1.80
	(1 sq m)	(0:12)	(0.90)		(2.00)

Don't forget, these prices may need adjustment depending on where you live.
Regional adjustments are provided on the inside cover, and further explanation is given in the Preface.

Plumbing

The introduction of plastic pipework and 'push-fit' joints in recent years means that you are now able to tackle many plumbing jobs that could previously only be carried out by an expert.

Repairs and alterations					
Remove 6 feet length of existing rainwater gutter and replace with new					
4″ (100 mm) half round cast iron	1 no	1:55	10.00	4	25.00
4½″ (115 mm) half round cast iron	1 no	2:00	10.50	4	27.00
4″ (100 mm) half round aluminium	1 no	1:25	10.50	4	18.00
4½″ (115 mm) half round plastic	1 no	1:30	4.00	4	14.00
Remove 6 feet length of existing rainwater pipe and replace with new					
2½″ (63 mm) diameter cast iron	1 no	1:50	16.00	4	30.00
3″ (75 mm) diameter cast iron	1 no	1:55	17.00	4	32.00
2½″ (63 mm) diameter aluminium	1 no	1:40	12.00	4	24.00
3″ (75 mm) diameter aluminium	1 no	1:45	14.00	4	26.00
2½″ (63 mm) diameter plastic	1 no	1:00	4.00	4	12.00
3″ (75 mm) diameter plastic	1 no	1:05	5.00	4	14.00
Cut out 2 feet length of copper pipe, insert new length and connect to existing pipe each end with compression fittings diameter					
15 mm	1 no	1:10	2.00	5	11.00
22 mm	1 no	1:20	3.00	5	13.00
28 mm	1 no	1:25	5.50	5	16.00
35 mm	1 no	1:30	11.00	5	22.00

Take off defective radiator valve and replace with new including draining down beforehand and bleeding system afterwards					
Single valves					
standard type	1 no	1:30	5.00	5	20.00
thermostatic type	1 no	1:30	12.00	5	30.00
Complete system (9 valves)					
standard type	1 no	6:00	45.00	5	110.00
thermostatic type	1 no	6:00	108.00	5	180.00
Take out existing central heating pump, replace with new, drain down and bleed system					
SMC Comet (130–145)	1 no	3:30	35.00	5	70.00
SMC Comet (160) bronze	1 no	3:30	70.00	5	115.00

Take out defective galvanised steel cold water storage tank and renew complete including connections to existing pipes					
15 gallon	1 no	6:00	30.00	5	70.00
25 gallon	1 no	7:00	40.00	5	100.00
40 gallon	1 no	8:00	60.00	5	135.00
Take off existing central heating radiator and refix in new position including re-using all existing materials	1 no	4:00	10.00	5	45.00
Take out existing sanitary fittings and renew including all necessary connections and taps					
new plastic bath (BP £120)	1 no	12:00	120.00	5	180.00
new wash basin (BP £55)	1 no	6:00	55.00	5	100.00
new low level WC suite (BP £140)	1 no	10:00	140.00	5	215.00

New work

Rainwater installation

Rainwater installation complete consisting of 112 mm plastic half round gutters and 75 mm diameter plastic down pipes including fittings					
terraced house	1 no	15:00	60.00	5	165.00
semi-detached house with gable end	1 no	15:00	75.00	5	180.00
semi-detached house with pitched end	1 no	18:00	95.00	5	215.00
detached house with gable ends	1 no	15:00	75.00	5	180.00
detached house with pitched ends	1 no	21:00	115.00	5	250.00

Don't forget, these prices may need adjustment depending on where you live.

Regional adjustments are provided on the inside cover, and further explanation is given in the Preface.

Rainwater installation complete consisting of 115 mm cast iron half round gutters and 75 mm diameter cast iron down pipes including fittings					
terraced house	1 no	20:00	290.00	5	420.00
semi-detached house with gable end	1 no	20:00	315.00	5	440.00
semi-detached house with pitched end	1 no	24:00	360.00	5	525.00
detached house with gable ends	1 no	20:00	315.00	5	440.00
detached house with pitched ends	1 no	30:00	420.00	5	580.00
Rainwater installation complete consisting of 113 mm aluminium gutters and 75 mm diameter aluminium down pipes including fittings					
terraced house	1 no	15:00	225.00	5	330.00
semi-detached house with gable end	1 no	15:00	245.00	5	365.00
semi-detached house with pitched end	1 no	18:00	280.00	5	440.00
detached house with gable ends	1 no	15:00	245.00	5	365.00
detached house with pitched ends	1 no	21:00	340.00	5	500.00

Pipework

Copper pipe with pre-soldered capillary joints and fittings					
15 mm diameter	1 m	0:30	1.20	6	3.00
forming bend with spring	1 no	0:15	–	6	1.00
elbow	1 no	0:30	0.30	6	2.00
tee	1 no	0:35	0.55	6	2.60
tap connector	1 no	0:30	0.80	6	2.90
22 mm diameter	1 m	0:35	2.00	6	4.50
forming bend with spring	1 no	0:20	–	6	1.25
elbow	1 no	0:30	0.60	6	2.25
tee	1 no	0:35	1.00	6	2.90
tap connector	1 no	0:30	1.25	6	3.50

28 mm diameter	1 m	0:45	2.30	6	5.00
forming bend with spring	1 no	0:25	–	6	1.60
elbow	1 no	0:35	1.15	6	3.20
tee	1 no	0:40	1.80	6	4.50
tap connector	1 no	0:50	3.20	6	6.50
Blue polyethylene pipes and fittings with fusion welded joints laid in trenches (digging trench not included here)					
25 mm diameter	1 m	0:20	0.60	6	2.00
tee	1 no	0:40	4.00	6	7.50
connection to copper pipe	1 no	0:30	2.40	6	5.00
Stopcock and valves					
Gunmetal stopcock with pre-soldered capillary joints					
15 mm diameter	1 no	0:30	2.00	6	4.50
22 mm diameter	1 no	0:35	3.20	6	6.00
28 mm diameter	1 no	0:40	8.20	6	12.00
Chromium plated hot and cold washing machine valve					
15 mm diameter	1 no	0:40	2.20	6	4.50
Cold water storage tanks					
Plastic tank to BS 4213 complete with lid					
4 gallons (18 litres)	1 no	1:30	8.00	5	25.00
15 gallons (68 litres)	1 no	1:30	20.00	5	35.00
20 gallons (91 litres)	1 no	1:30	24.00	5	40.00
25 gallons (114 litres)	1 no	2:00	28.00	5	50.00
40 gallons (182 litres)	1 no	2:00	40.00	5	65.00
50 gallons (227 litres)	1 no	2:30	45.00	5	70.00
Cylinders					
Indirect copper cylinders to BS 699 grade 3					
ref 1, 21 gallons (96 litres)	1 no	1:30	45.00	5	70.00
ref 2, 25 gallons (114 litres)	1 no	1:30	48.00	5	75.00
ref 7, 31 gallons (140 litres)	1 no	1:30	50.00	5	80.00

Primatic single feed indirect copper cylinder, ready insulated					
20 gallons (92 litres)	1 no	1:30	90.00	5	130.00
24 gallons (108 litres)	1 no	1:30	95.00	5	140.00
Combination indirect single feed copper cylinder to BS 3198					
450 mm diameter × 900 mm high 19 gallons (85 litres) hot capacity and 5.5 gallons (25 litres) cold capacity	1 no	1:30	120.00	5	160.00
450 mm diameter × 1200 mm high 25 gallons (115 litres) hot capacity and 10 gallons (45 litres) cold capacity	1 no	1:30	135.00	5	175.00
Insulation					
Cistern jacket in glass fibre with polythene cover with two fixing bands					
635 × 457 × 483 mm	1 no	1:20	6.00	3	12.00
686 × 533 × 533 mm	1 no	1:30	7.00	3	14.00
737 × 584 × 508 mm	1 no	1:40	8.00	3	15.00
Hot water cylinder jacket in glass fibre with PVC cover with two fixing bands for cylinder size					
450 mm diameter × 900 mm high	1 no	0:30	9.00	3	14.00
450 mm diameter × 1050 mm high	1 no	0:35	12.00	3	18.00
450 mm diameter × 1200 mm high	1 no	0:40	14.00	3	20.00
Pre-formed pipe lagging in fire retardant foam 13 mm thick to pipe size					
15 mm diameter	1 m	0:10	1.00	3	2.00
22 mm diameter	1 m	0:12	1.20	3	2.25
28 mm diameter	1 m	0:15	1.30	3	2.50

Waste pipes and traps					
uPVC pipes and fittings fixing to walls					
32 mm diameter	1 m	0:40	2.30	5	5.00
bend	1 no	0:35	1.20	5	3.50
tee	1 no	0:40	1.50	5	4.50
connection to gully	1 no	0:30	1.40	5	4.00
40 mm diameter	1 m	0:45	3.00	5	6.00
bend	1 no	0:40	1.50	5	4.00
tee	1 no	0:45	1.80	5	5.00
connection to gully	1 no	0:35	1.75	5	4.50
50 mm diameter	1 m	0:50	4.00	5	6.50
bend	1 no	0:45	1.80	5	4.75
tee	1 no	0:50	3.00	5	6.50
connection to gully	1 no	0:40	2.00	5	5.00
Polypropylene traps with screwed joints to fitting outlet and pipe					
bottle P trap					
32 mm	1 no	0:45	2.20	4	5.00
40 mm	1 no	0:50	2.50	4	6.00
bottle S trap					
32 mm	1 no	0:45	2.40	4	5.50
40 mm	1 no	0:50	3.00	4	6.50
tubular bath trap					
P trap	1 no	1:00	4.50	4	8.00
S trap	1 no	1:00	5.50	4	9.00
Soil and vent pipes					
110 mm diameter uPVC Terrain System 100, solvent welded joints fixed to brickwork with holderbats at average 1250 mm centres	1 m	0:45	5.00	5	11.00
access bend	1 no	0:45	11.00	5	20.00
single branch	1 no	0:45	6.00	5	15.00
single branch with access	1 no	0:45	13.00	5	22.00
double branch	1 no	0:50	17.00	5	25.00
W.C. connecting bend	1 no	0:35	6.00	5	14.00
W.C. connector	1 no	0:35	3.50	5	10.00

Sanitary fittings					
Acrylic bath 1700 mm long complete with 2 chromium plated grips (excluding taps)					
white	1 no	4:00	80.00	6	130.00
coloured	1 no	4:00	90.00	6	140.00
Polystyrene bath panel					
end	1 no	0:40	9.00	4	14.00
side	1 no	0:50	15.00	4	20.00
Polished aluminium angle strip screwed to corner of bath panels					
25 × 25 mm	1 no	0:30	2.00	4	4.00
Vitreous china white wash basin complete (excluding taps) size 560 × 430 mm					
fixed to wall brackets	1 no	2:30	25.00	6	45.00
pedestal mounted	1 no	2:30	40.00	6	60.00
Vitreous china coloured wash basin complete (excluding taps) size 560 × 430 mm					
fixed to wall brackets	1 no	2:30	30.00	6	50.00
pedestal mounted	1 no	2:30	50.00	6	70.00
White close coupled W.C. suite with plastic seat, 9 litre cistern, ball valve, flush pipe and connect to drain outlet					
washdown type	1 no	3:30	100.00	6	160.00
syphonic type	1 no	3:30	190.00	6	245.00
Coloured close coupled W.C. suite with plastic seat, 9 litre cistern, ball valve, flush pipe and connect to drain outlet					
washdown type	1 no	3:30	140.00	6	195.00
syphonic type	1 no	3:30	220.00	6	275.00
Vitreous china freestanding bidet (excluding fittings)					
white	1 no	3:30	70.00	6	110.00
coloured	1 no	3:30	95.00	6	130.00

Stainless steel sink tops complete (excluding taps)					
single bowl and single drainer size 1000 × 500 mm	1 no	2:00	125.00	5	155.00
single bowl and double drainer size 1500 × 500 mm	1 no	2:30	150.00	5	180.00
double bowl with single drainer size 1500 × 500 mm	1 no	2:30	200.00	5	240.00
Taps					
Chromium plated wash basin, sink and bath pillar taps					
½″ diameter	1 pair	1:00	12.00	6	18.00
⅜″ diameter	1 pair	1:00	15.00	6	22.00
Chromium plated bath mixer taps complete with handspray	1 no	1:00	40.00	6	60.00
Chromium plated sink mixer taps with swivel spout	1 no	1:00	35.00	6	55.00
Showers					
Thermostatic mixing valve fixing to wall	1 no	1:00	110.00	6	135.00
Mechanical mixing valve fixing to wall	1 no	1:00	55.00	6	75.00
Flexible tube and handspray with sliding bar attachment	1 no	1:00	28.00	6	45.00
Glazed fireclay shower tray fixed to floor					
white	1 no	2:00	95.00	5	140.00
coloured	1 no	2:00	100.00	5	150.00
Acrylic shower tray fixed to floor					
white	1 no	1:50	40.00	5	65.00
coloured	1 no	1:50	40.00	5	65.00

Don't forget, these prices may need adjustment depending on where you live.
Regional adjustments are provided on the inside cover, and further explanation is given in the Preface.

Central heating

Radiators					
Steel single panel radiator fixed to bracket plugged to wall					
480 × 450 mm high	1 no	2:00	15.00	6	30.00
1120 × 450 mm high	1 no	2:20	25.00	6	45.00
1920 × 450 mm high	1 no	2:30	40.00	6	65.00
480 × 750 mm high	1 no	2:20	20.00	6	40.00
1120 × 750 mm high	1 no	2:30	40.00	6	60.00
1920 × 750 mm high	1 no	2:45	80.00	6	110.00
Steel double panel radiator fixed to brackets plugged to wall					
800 × 450 mm high	1 no	2:20	35.00	6	55.00
1280 × 450 mm high	1 no	2:40	55.00	6	85.00
1920 × 450 mm high	1 no	3:00	75.00	6	120.00
640 × 750 mm high	1 no	2:40	40.00	6	65.00
1120 × 750 mm high	1 no	3:00	70.00	6	110.00
1760 × 750 mm high	1 no	3:30	145.00	6	200.00
Valves					
Thermostatic radiator valves					
15 mm diameter	1 no	0:45	12.00	6	20.00
Boilers					
Boilers (for central heating and indirect hot water)					
Solid fuel boiler, gravity feed, white stove enamelled casing, thermostat, 125 mm flue socket					
13.2 kWh output	1 no	10:00	580.00	7	750.00
17.6 kWh output	1 no	10:00	675.00	7	840.00
Oil fired boiler, fully automatic, white stove enamelled casing, for Kerosene or gas oil, conventional flue					
16–19 kWh output	1 no	9:00	500.00	7	680.00
20.5–26.4 kWh output	1 no	9:00	550.00	7	740.00
27.9–35.2 kWh output	1 no	9:00	600.00	7	800.00

Gas fired boiler, Potterton Kingfisher range, free standing					
type CF40	1 no	8:00	270.00	7	360.00
type CF60	1 no	8:00	300.00	7	390.00
type CF100	1 no	8:00	440.00	7	540.00
type RS100 with balanced flue	1 no	8:00	600.00	7	800.00
Gas fired boiler, Glow worm space saver range, wall mounted, balanced flue					
type 30B	1 no	8:00	240.00	7	330.00
type 40B	1 no	8:00	280.00	7	370.00
type 50B	1 no	8:00	300.00	7	390.00
type 60B	1 no	8:00	360.00	7	460.00
type 80B	1 no	8:00	540.00	7	730.00

Don't forget, these prices may need adjustment depending on where you live.
Regional adjustments are provided on the inside cover, and further explanation is given in the Preface.

Shelving

'Putting up shelves' is one of the most common of all DIY activities. Not only is it a reasonably simple task but it also can be very satisfying to use the shelves within minutes of completing the work!

Softwood shelving bearers plugged and screwed to brick or blockwork wall					
19 × 50 mm	1 m	0:15	0.50	5	1.50
25 × 50 mm	1 m	0:15	0.60	5	1.65
Softwood shelving 19 mm thick fixed to bearers, width					
150 mm	1 m	0:20	1.30	5	4.20
225 mm	1 m	0:25	1.80	5	4.80
300 mm	1 m	0:30	2.30	5	5.40
Birch faced blockboard fixed to bearers, size					
16 × 150 mm	1 m	0:20	1.50	5	3.60
16 × 225 mm	1 m	0:25	2.30	5	4.50
22 × 150 mm	1 m	0:20	2.00	5	4.10
22 × 225 mm	1 m	0:25	2.75	5	5.00
25 × 150 mm	1 m	0:25	2.20	5	4.40
25 × 225 mm	1 m	0:30	3.10	5	5.40
Birch faced plywood fixed to bearers, size					
6 × 150 mm	1 m	0:15	0.90	5	2.80
12 × 150 mm	1 m	0:15	1.30	5	3.20
15 × 150 mm	1 m	0:20	1.50	5	3.60
19 × 150 mm	1 m	0:20	1.80	5	3.90
6 × 225 mm	1 m	0:22	1.20	5	3.00
12 × 225 mm	1 m	0:22	2.00	5	4.15
15 × 225 mm	1 m	0:25	2.25	5	4.40
19 × 225 mm	1 m	0:25	2.60	5	4.80

Chipboard fixed to bearers, size					
12 × 150 mm	1 m	0:15	0.50	5	2.40
18 × 150 mm	1 m	0:20	0.60	5	2.60
25 × 150 mm	1 m	0:25	0.80	5	3.00
12 × 225 mm	1 m	0:22	0.75	5	2.90
18 × 225 mm	1 m	0:25	0.90	5	3.15
25 × 225 mm	1 m	0:30	1.10	5	3.40
Plastic faced blockboard fixed to bearers, size					
16 × 150 mm	1 m	0:20	9.00	5	13.00
18 × 150 mm	1 m	0:20	9.20	5	13.30
22 × 150 mm	1 m	0:25	9.40	5	13.75
25 × 150 mm	1 m	0:25	9.60	5	14.10
16 × 225 mm	1 m	0:25	11.50	5	16.00
18 × 225 mm	1 m	0:25	11.75	5	16.25
22 × 225 mm	1 m	0:30	12.25	5	17.50
25 × 225 mm	1 m	0:30	12.50	5	18.00

Don't forget, these prices may need adjustment depending on where you live.
Regional adjustments are provided on the inside cover, and further explanation is given in the Preface.

Flooring

Floor finishes have been dealt with earlier so this section covers the joists and the various types of boarding. If you are laying joists to a new floor (as opposed to replacing a defective joist) you should take advice on the size of joist necessary to carry the superimposed weight. Don't guess!

Softwood flooring joists					
50 × 75 mm	1 m	0:10	1.00	4	2.50
50 × 100 mm	1 m	0:12	1.30	4	2.90
50 × 125 mm	1 m	0:15	1.50	4	3.30
75 × 150 mm	1 m	0:20	2.60	4	3.90
75 × 175 mm	1 m	0:25	3.30	4	5.00
75 × 200 mm	1 m	0:30	3.75	4	5.60
Softwood flooring joists impregnated with preservative under pressure					
50 × 75 mm	1 m	0:10	1.10	4	2.70
50 × 100 mm	1 m	0:12	1.45	4	3.10
50 × 125 mm	1 m	0:15	1.65	4	3.50
75 × 150 mm	1 m	0:20	2.80	4	4.15
75 × 175 mm	1 m	0:25	3.60	4	5.40
75 × 200 mm	1 m	0:30	4.10	4	6.20
Softwood butt jointed boarding nailed to joists, size					
19 × 75 mm	1 sq m	1:00	8.50	5	17.00
25 × 100 mm	1 sq m	1:10	9.50	5	18.20
Softwood tongued and grooved boarding nailed to joists, size					
19 × 125 mm	1 sq m	1:20	9.50	5	18.40
25 × 150 mm	1 sq m	1:30	10.50	5	19.70
Softwood butt jointed boarding nailed to joists, size					
18 mm thick	1 sq m	0:30	3.60	5	7.00
22 mm thick	1 sq m	0:35	5.60	5	9.50

Chipboard boarding tongued and grooved joints, nailed to joists, size					
18 mm thick	1 sq m	0:35	3.80	5	7.50
22 mm thick	1 sq m	0:40	5.80	5	10.40
Plywood boarding, tongued and grooved joints, nailed to joists					
15 mm thick	1 sq m	0:35	12.00	5	17.00
18 mm thick	1 sq m	0:40	13.00	5	18.40

Don't forget, these prices may need adjustment depending on where you live.
Regional adjustments are provided on the inside cover, and further explanation is given in the Preface.

Glazing repairs

The first part of this section deals with glazing repairs and covers the replacement of broken windows that most householders suffer from occasionally. Although the glazing industry normally works in square metres, sample pane sizes have been given to make the figures quoted more helpful.

Clear glass 4 mm thick					
Hack out broken glass from wood or metal windows and reglaze in putty, size					
6″ × 12″ (150 × 300 mm)	1 no	0:50	1.40	4	3.00
9″ × 18″ (225 × 450 mm)	1 no	0:55	2.30	4	5.00
18″ × 18″ (450 × 450 mm)	1 no	1:00	4.20	4	7.00
30″ × 24″ (750 × 600 mm)	1 no	1:05	9.75	4	12.00
36″ × 30″ (900 × 750 mm)	1 no	1:10	11.50	4	16.00
Hack out broken glass from wood or metal windows and reglaze in pinned beads previously laid aside					
6″ × 12″ (150 × 300 mm)	1 no	0:40	1.30	4	3.50
9″ × 18″ (225 × 450 mm)	1 no	0:50	2.15	4	5.70
18″ × 18″ (450 × 450 mm)	1 no	0:55	4.00	4	8.00
30″ × 24″ (750 × 600 mm)	1 no	1:00	9.25	4	13.50
36″ × 30″ (900 × 750 mm)	1 no	1:05	11.00	4	17.50
Obscure glass 6 mm thick					
Hack out broken glass from wood or metal windows and reglaze in putty, size					
6″ × 12″ (150 × 300 mm)	1 no	0:50	2.25	4	4.60
9″ × 18″ (225 × 450 mm)	1 no	0:55	3.00	4	7.60
18″ × 18″ (450 × 450 mm)	1 no	1:00	6.20	4	10.00
30″ × 24″ (750 × 600 mm)	1 no	1:05	13.40	4	17.25
36″ × 30″ (900 × 750 mm)	1 no	1:10	17.50	4	23.00

Hack out broken glass from wood or metal windows and reglaze in pinned beads previously laid aside					
6″ × 12″ (150 × 300 mm)	1 no	0:40	2.10	4	5.00
9″ × 18″ (225 × 450 mm)	1 no	0:50	2.80	4	8.20
18″ × 18″ (450 × 450 mm)	1 no	0:55	5.80	4	11.00
30″ × 24″ (750 × 600 mm)	1 no	1:00	12.90	4	19.40
36″ × 30″ (900 × 750 mm)	1 no	1:05	16.75	4	24.50

Double glazing

The cost of having double glazing fitted at the factory is given in the 'Windows' section but the prices are only applicable when you are also having a new window fitted. The following prices refer to double glazing fitted in your existing wood windows and include the cost of removing the existing glass and cleaning the rebates.

Note that the price per square metre varies considerably depending upon the size of pane and these have been grouped into 3 categories:

Small	not exceeding 5 square feet (approximately ½ square metre)
Medium	between 5 and 10 square feet (approximately ½ to 1 square metre)
Large	over 10 square feet (approximately 1 square metre)

Description	Quantity	Contractor's price £
Hermetically sealed double glazing units consisting of two panes of 4 mm thick clear sheet glass fixed to wood in putty and sprigs in panes		
small	1 sq yd	56.00
	(1 sq m)	(62.00)
medium	1 sq yd	45.00
	(1 sq m)	(50.00)
large	1 sq yd	40.00
	(1 sq m)	(45.00)

Description	Quantity	Contractor's price £
Hermetically sealed double glazing units consisting of two panes of 4 mm thick clear sheet glass fixed to wood with screwed beads in panes size		
small	1 sq yd	59.00
	(1 sq m)	(65.00)
medium	1 sq yd	48.00
	(1 sq m)	(54.00)
large	1 sq yd	45.00
	(1 sq m)	(50.00)
Hermetically sealed double glazing units consisting of two panes of 6 mm thick clear sheet glass fixed to wood in putty and sprigs in panes		
small	1 sq yd	66.00
	(1 sq m)	(72.00)
medium	1 sq yd	59.00
	(1 sq m)	(64.00)
large	1 sq yd	55.00
	(1 sq m)	(60.00)
Hermetically sealed double glazing units consisting of two panes of 6 mm thick clear sheet glass fixed to wood with screwed beads in panes size		
small	1 sq yd	69.00
	(1 sq m)	(76.00)
medium	1 sq yd	61.00
	(1 sq m)	(68.00)
large	1 sq yd	56.00
	(1 sq m)	(63.00)

Electric installation

Carrying out electrical work is a mixture of basic DIY skills – lifting floorboards, drilling holes in walls and ceilings – and highly technical tasks which are better left to the professional. Because of this combination of different levels of skills, the prices quoted below are for having the work done by a contractor and are based upon working in situations where there are no major obstructions to the most economical use of cable runs.

Description	Quantity	Contractor's price £
Form spur from existing point not exceeding 10 feet (3. 3 m) distance to provide		
single 13 amp power point	1 no	35.00
twin 13 amp power point	1 no	40.00
lighting point with flex and lamp holder	1 no	30.00
shaver point	1 no	50.00
cooker point control unit	1 no	70.00
TV socket outlet	1 no	30.00
telephone outlet	1 no	28.00
dimmer switch	1 no	55.00
bell push	1 no	30.00
3.4 kW floor mounted storage heater	1 no	250.00
4 kW infra red heater	1 no	130.00
3 kW twin thermostat heater	1 no	60.00
Window extractor fan	1 no	135.00

Don't forget, these prices may need adjustment depending on where you live.
Regional adjustments are provided on the inside cover, and further explanation is given in the Preface.

Description	Quantity	Contractor's price £
Form spur from existing point not exceeding 20 feet (6. 6 m) distance to provide		
single 13 amp power point	1 no	40.00
twin 13 amp power point	1 no	45.00
lighting point with flex and lamp holder	1 no	33.00
shaver point	1 no	55.00
cooker point control unit	1 no	75.00
TV socket outlet	1 no	35.00
telephone outlet	1 no	33.00
dimmer switch	1 no	60.00
bell push	1 no	35.00
3.4 kW floor mounted storage heater	1 no	255.00
4 kW infra red heater	1 no	135.00
3 kW twin thermostat heater	1 no	65.00
window extractor fan	1 no	140.00

Description	Quantity	Contractor's price £
Supply and fix single tube fluorescent light fittings to adjacent ceiling lighting point		
600 mm long	1 no	25.00
1200 mm long	1 no	28.00
1500 mm long	1 no	30.00
1800 mm long	1 no	38.00
2400 mm long	1 no	45.00
Supply and fix twin tube fluorescent light fittings to adjacent ceiling lighting point		
600 mm long	1 no	35.00
1200 mm long	1 no	42.00
1500 mm long	1 no	50.00
1800 mm long	1 no	55.00
2400 mm long	1 no	70.00

Don't forget, these prices may need adjustment depending on where you live.
Regional adjustments are provided on the inside cover, and further explanation is given in the Preface.

Decorating and paperhanging

Painting and decorating is probably the most popular of all DIY activities. Everybody sees themselves as capable of painting although the standards achieved vary widely. This section is divided into two parts. The first gives square yard and square metre prices and other information and the second shows the areas of surfaces to be painted or papered in standard size rooms together with illustrations of the cost of carrying out the work and the hours involved. The basic price (BP) of wallpaper shown is the normal retail price. All the information given in this section is based upon the use of brushes. If you decide to use spraying equipment you could probably achieve a 30%–50% saving on labour but would use an extra 10% to 20% material.

Internal painting
Table 1

Existing work					
Scrape off one layer of wallpaper from					
plastered walls	1 sq yd (1 sq m)	0:25 (0:30)	–	2	1.25 (1.40)
plastered ceilings	1 sq yd (1 sq m)	0:35 (0:40)	–	2	1.80 (2.00)
Scrape off two layers of wallpaper from					
plastered walls	1 sq yd (1 sq m)	0:35 (0:40)	–	2	1.80 (2.00)
plastered ceilings	1 sq yd (1 sq m)	0:45 (0:50)	–	2	2.30 (2.50)
Wash down previously painted surfaces and rub down, width					
over 12″ (300 mm)	1 sq yd (1 sq m)	0:20 (0:22)	–	2	1.50 (1.65)
6″–12″ (150–300 mm)	1 yd (1 m)	0:08 (0:09)	–	2	0.50 (0.55)
not exceeding 6″ (150 mm)	1 yd (1 m)	0:03 (0:04)	–	2	0.20 (0:22)

Burn off existing paint from general surfaces, width					
over 12″ (300 mm)	1 sq yd	1:15	–	3	6.50
	(1 sq m)	(1:20)			(6.75)
6″–12″ (150–300 mm)	1 yd	0:30	–	3	1.40
	(1 m)	(0:35)			(1.80)
not exceeding 6″ (150 mm)	1 yd	0:20	–	3	1.50
	(1 m)	(0:22)			(1.65)
New work					
Walls and ceilings					
One coat alkali resisting primer on					
brickwork	1 sq yd	0:17	0.27	5	1.55
	(1 sq m)	(0:19)	(0.30)		(1.70)
blockwork	1 sq yd	0:22	0.36	5	1.90
	(1 sq m)	(0:25)	(0.40)		(2.10)
concrete walls	1 sq yd	0:14	0.21	5	1.35
	(1 sq m)	(0:16)	(0.24)		(1.50)
concrete ceilings	1 sy yd	0:18	0.21	5	1.55
	(1 sq m)	(0:21)	(0.24)		(1.70)
plastered walls	1 sq yd	0:12	0.21	5	1.28
	(1 sq m)	(0:14)	(0.24)		(1.40)
plastered ceilings	1 sq yd	0:14	0.21	5	1.45
	(1 sq m)	(0:16)	(0.24)		(1.60)
One coat emulsion paint on					
brickwork	1 sq yd	0:15	0.22	5	1.30
	(1 sq m)	(0:18)	(0.24)		(1.45)
blockwork	1 sq yd	0:20	0.27	5	1.60
	(1 sq m)	(0:23)	(0.30)		(1.75)
concrete walls	1 sq yd	0:12	0.15	5	1.00
	(1 sq m)	(0:14)	(0.18)		(1.10)
concrete ceilings	1 sq yd	0:15	0.15	5	1.30
	(1 sq m)	(0:18)	(0.18)		(1.45)
plastered walls	1 sq yd	0:10	0.15	5	0.95
	(1 sq m)	(0:12)	(0.18)		(1.05)
plastered ceilings	1 sq yd	0:12	0.15	5	1.20
	(1 sq m)	(0:14)	(0.18)		(1.30)

Woodwork					
One coat wood primer on general surfaces, width					
over 12″ (300 mm)	1 sq yd	0:20	0.34	5	2.00
	(1 sq m)	(0:22)	(0.38)		(2.20)
6″–12″ (150–300 mm)	1 yd	0:05	0.13	5	1.05
	(1 m)	(0:06)	(0.15)		(1.15)
not exceeding 6″ (150 mm)	1 yd	0:02	0.07	5	0.80
	(1 m)	(0:03)	(0.08)		(0.90)
One coat oil based undercoat on general surfaces, width					
over 12″ (300 mm)	1 sq yd	0:20	0.30	5	1.90
	(1 sq m)	(0:22)	(0.33)		(2.10)
6″–12″ (150–300 mm)	1 yd	0:05	0.12	5	1.00
	(1 m)	(0:06)	(0.14)		(1.10)
not exceeding 6″ (150 mm)	1 yd	0:02	0.06	5	0.75
	(1 m)	(0:03)	(0.07)		(0.85)
One coat oil based gloss on general surfaces, width					
over 12″ (300 mm)	1 sq yd	0:20	0.30	5	1.95
	(1 sq m)	(0:22)	(0.33)		(2.15)
6″–12″ (150–300 mm)	1 yd	0:05	0.12	5	1.05
	(1 m)	(0:06)	(0.14)		(1.15)
not exceeding 6″ (150 mm)	1 yd	0:02	0.06	5	0.80
	(1 m)	(0:03)	(0.07)		(0.90)
Metalwork					
One coat metal primer on general surfaces, width					
over 12″ (300 mm)	1 sq yd	0:20	0.35	5	2.00
	(1 sq m)	(0:22)	(0.40)		(2.20)
6″–12″ (150–300 mm)	1 yd	0:05	0.15	5	1.05
	(1 m)	(0:06)	(0.17)		(1.15)
not exceeding 6″ (150 mm)	1 yd	0:02	0.08	5	0.80
	(1 m)	(0:03)	(0.09)		(0.90)
One coat oil based undercoat on general surfaces, width					
over 12″ (300 mm)	1 sq yd	0:20	0.30	5	1.90
	(1 sq m)	(0:22)	(0.33)		(2.10)
6″–12″ (150–300 mm)	1 yd	0:05	0.12	5	1.00
	(1 m)	(0:06)	(0.14)		(1.10)
not exceeding 6″ (150 mm)	1 yd	0:02	0.06	5	0.75
	(1 m)	(0:03)	(0:07)		(0.85)

One coat oil based gloss on general surfaces, width					
over 12″ (300 mm)	1 sq yd	0:20	0:30	5	1.95
	(1 sq m)	(0:22)	(0.32)		(2.15)
6″–12″ (150–300 mm)	1 yd	0:05	0:12	5	1.05
	(1 m)	(0:06)	(0.14)		(1.15)
not exceeding 6″ (150 mm)	1 yd	0:02	0.06	5	0.80
	(1 m)	(0:03)	(0.07)		(0.90)
Stains and varnishes					
Prepare and apply two coats 'Cuprinol' oak preserver on general surfaces, width					
over 12″ (300 mm)	1 sq yd	0:25	0.70	5	3.00
	(1 sq m)	(0:28)	(0.80)		(3.30)
6″–12″ (150–300 mm)	1 yd	0:16	0.25	5	2.00
	(1 m)	(0:18)	(0.28)		(2.20)
not exceeding 6″ (150 mm)	1 yd	0:10	0.15	5	1.20
	(1 m)	(0:11)	(0.12)		(1.35)
Prepare and apply two coats clear polyurethene on general surfaces, width					
over 12″ (300 mm)	1 sq yd	0:27	0.75	5	3.20
	(1 sq m)	(0:30)	(0.85)		(3.50)
6″–12″ (150–300 mm)	1 yd	0:18	0.28	5	2.10
	(1 m)	(0:20)	(0.32)		(2.30)
not exceeding 6″ (150 mm)	1 yd	0:12	0.18	5	1.25
	(1 m)	(0:14)	(0.20)		(1.40)

Wallpapering

The basic price referred to (BP) is the purchase cost of the paper per roll. The net materials column contains an allowance for paste and filling materials for cracks and also for waste. For every 50p variation

Don't forget, these prices may need adjustment depending on where you live.
Regional adjustments are provided on the inside cover, and further explanation is given in the Preface.

in the basic price per roll, the material column should be increased or decreased by 12p per square yard (14p per square metre.)

Hang wallpaper to walls					
lining paper (BP £0.70)	1 sq yd	0:17	0.15	6	1.50
	(1 sq m)	(0:20)	(0.17)		(1.80)
woodchip paper (BP £0.80)	1 sq yd	0:17	0.16	6	1.60
	(1 sq m)	(0:20)	(0.19)		(1.90)
flock paper (BP £6.00)	1 sq yd	0:20	1.15	6	2.60
	(1 sq m)	(0:25)	(1.40)		(3.10)
Anaglypta paper (BP £1.50)	1 sq yd	0:20	0.20	6	1.65
	(1 sq m)	(0:25)	(0.35)		(2.00)
standard patterned paper	1 sq yd	0:20	0.90	6	2.30
(BP £4.50)	(1 sq m)	(0:25)	(1.06)		(2.80)
vinyl surface paper	1 sq yd	0:20	1.10	6	2.50
(BP £5.50)	(1 sq m)	(0:25)	(1.30)		(3.00)
Hang wallpaper to ceilings					
lining paper (BP £0.70)	1 sq yd	0:20	0.15	6	2.30
	(1 sq m)	(0:25)	(0.17)		(2.00)
woodchip paper (BP £0.80)	1 sq yd	0:20	0.16	6	1.75
	(1 sq m)	(0:25)	(0.19)		(2.10)
flock paper (BP £6.00)	1 sq yd	0:20	1.15	6	2.75
	(1 sq m)	(0:25)	(1.40)		(3.30)
Anaglypta paper (BP £1.50)	1 sq yd	0:20	0.30	6	1.90
	(1 sq m)	(0:25)	(0.35)		(2.30)
standard patterned paper	1 sq yd	0:20	0.90	6	2.50
(BP £4.50)	(1 sq m)	(0:25)	(1.06)		(3.00)
vinyl surface paper	1 sq yd	0:20	1.10	6	2.65
(BP £5.50)	(1 sq m)	(0:25)	(1.30)		(3.20)

Table 2 shows the net areas and lengths of surfaces to be painted or papered in the average house. The following assumptions have been made:

Living room	1 door, 1 fireplace, 1 large window;
Dining room	2 doors, 1 large window;
Bedroom	1 door, 1 average window;
Kitchen	2 doors, fittings below dado height, 1 large window;
W.C.	1 door, 1 small window;
Bathroom	1 door, 1 cupboard, 1 average window.
Ceiling heights	Ground floor 7′9″ (2.4 m);
	First floor 7′6″ (2.2 m).

Table 2

	Ceiling	Walls	Window	Door	Skirting	Frames
Living room						
12′ × 10′ (3.6 × 3.0 m)	13 sq yd (11 sq m)	29 sq yd (24 sq m)	3 sq yd (3 sq m)	2 sq yd (2 sq m)	11 yd (10 m)	10 yd (8 m)
12′ × 12′ (3.6 × 3.6 m)	16 sq yd (13 sq m)	31 sq yd (26 sq m)	3 sq yd (3 sq m)	2 sq yd (2 sq m)	12 yd (11 m)	10 yd (8 m)
14′ × 10′ (4.2 × 3.0 m)	16 sq yd (13 sq m)	31 sq yd (26 sq m)	3 sq yd (3 sq m)	2 sq yd (2 sq m)	12 yd (11 m)	10 yd (8 m)
14′ × 12′ (4.2 × 3.6 m)	19 sq yd (15 sq m)	35 sq yd (29 sq m)	3 sq yd (3 sq m)	2 sq yd (2 sq m)	14 yd (13 m)	10 yd (8 m)
14′ × 14′ (4.2 × 4.2 m)	22 sq yd (18 sq m)	38 sq yd (32 sq m)	3 sq yd (3 sq m)	2 sq yd (2 sq m)	15 yd (14 m)	10 yd (8 m)
16′ × 10′ (4.8 × 3.0 m)	18 sq yd (15 sq m)	35 sq yd (29 sq m)	3 sq yd (3 sq m)	2 sq yd (2 sq m)	14 yd (13 m)	10 yd (8 m)
16′ × 12′ (4.8 × 3.6 m)	21 sq yd (17 sq m)	38 sq yd (32 sq m)	3 sq yd (3 sq m)	2 sq yd (2 sq m)	15 yd (14 m)	10 yd (8 m)
16′ × 14′ (4.8 × 4.2 m)	25 sq yd (20 sq m)	41 sq yd (34 sq m)	3 sq yd (3 sq m)	2 sq yd (2 sq m)	17 yd (15 m)	10 yd (8 m)
16′ × 16′ (4.8 × 4.8 m)	28 sq yd (23 sq m)	44 sq yd (37 sq m)	3 sq yd (3 sq m)	2 sq yd (2 sq m)	18 yd (16 m)	10 yd (8 m)
Dining room						
10′ × 10′ (3.0 × 3.0 m)	11 sq yd (9 sq m)	24 sq yd (20 sq m)	3 sq yd (3 sq m)	4 sq yd (4 sq m)	11 yd (10 m)	16 yd (13 m)
12′ × 10′ (3.6 × 3.0 m)	13 sq yd (11 sq m)	29 sq yd (24 sq m)	3 sq yd (3 sq m)	4 sq yd (4 sq m)	12 yd (11 m)	16 yd (13 m)
12′ × 12′ (3.6 × 3.6 m)	16 sq yd (13 sq m)	31 sq yd (26 sq m)	3 sq yd (3 sq m)	4 sq yd (4 sq m)	14 yd (13 m)	16 yd (13 m)
14′ × 10′ (4.2 × 3.0 m)	16 sq yd (13 sq m)	31 sq yd (26 sq m)	3 sq yd (3 sq m)	4 sq yd (4 sq m)	14 yd (13 m)	16 yd (13 m)
14′ × 12′ (4.2 × 3.6 m)	19 sq yd (15 sq m)	35 sq yd (29 sq m)	3 sq yd (3 sq m)	4 sq yd (4 sq m)	17 yd (15 m)	16 yd (13 m)
14′ × 14′ (4.2 × 4.2 m)	22 sq yd (18 sq m)	38 sq yd (32 sq m)	3 sq yd (3 sq m)	4 sq yd (4 sq m)	18 yd (16 m)	16 yd (13 m)
16′ × 10′ (4.8 × 3.0 m)	18 sq yd (15 sq m)	35 sq yd (29 sq m)	3 sq yd (3 sq m)	4 sq yd (4 sq m)	17 yd (15 m)	16 yd (13 m)
16′ × 12′ (4.8 × 3.6 m)	21 sq yd (17 sq m)	38 sq yd (32 sq m)	3 sq yd (3 sq m)	4 sq yd (4 sq m)	18 yd (16 m)	16 yd (13 m)
16′ × 14′ (4.8 × 4.2 m)	25 sq yd (20 sq m)	41 sq yd (34 sq m)	3 sq yd (3 sq m)	4 sq yd (4 sq m)	19 yd (17 m)	16 yd (13 m)
Bedroom						
8′ × 8′ (2.4 × 2.4 m)	7 sq yd (6 sq m)	20 sq yd (17 sq m)	2 sq yd (2 sq m)	2 sq yd (2 sq m)	10 yd (8 m)	8 yd (7 m)
8′ × 10′ (2.4 × 3.0 m)	9 sq yd (7 sq m)	24 sq yd (20 sq m)	2 sq yd (2 sq m)	2 sq yd (2 sq m)	11 yd (10 m)	8 yd (7 m)
8′ × 12′ (2.4 × 3.6 m)	11 sq yd (9 sq m)	26 sq yd (22 sq m)	2 sq yd (2 sq m)	2 sq yd (2 sq m)	12 yd (11 m)	8 yd (7 m)
10′ × 10′ (3.0 × 3.0 m)	11 sq yd (9 sq m)	26 sq yd (22 sq m)	2 sq yd (2 sq m)	2 sq yd (2 sq m)	12 yd (11 m)	8 yd (7 m)

	Ceiling	Walls	Window	Door	Skirting	Frames
10′ × 12′ (3.0 × 3.6 m)	13 sq yd (11 sq m)	30 sq yd (25 sq m)	2 sq yd (2 sq m)	2 sq yd (2 sq m)	13 yd (12 m)	8 yd (7 m)
12′ × 12′ (3.6 × 3.6 m)	16 sq yd (13 sq m)	32 sq yd (27 sq m)	2 sq yd (2 sq m)	2 sq yd (2 sq m)	14 yd (13 m)	8 yd (7 m)
12′ × 14′ (3.6 × 4.2 m)	19 sq yd (15 sq m)	36 sq yd (30 sq m)	2 sq yd (2 sq m)	2 sq yd (2 sq m)	17 yd (15 m)	8 yd (7 m)
12′ × 16′ (3.6 × 4.8 m)	21 sq yd (17 sq m)	38 sq yd (32 sq m)	2 sq yd (2 sq m)	2 sq yd (2 sq m)	18 yd (16 m)	8 yd (7 m)
14′ × 14′ (4.2 × 4.2 m)	22 sq yd (18 sq m)	38 sq yd (32 sq m)	2 sq yd (2 sq m)	2 sq yd (2 sq m)	18 yd (16 m)	8 yd (7 m)
14′ × 16′ (4.2 × 4.8 m)	25 sq yd (20 sq m)	42 sq yd (35 sq m)	2 sq yd (2 sq m)	2 sq yd (2 sq m)	19 yd (17 m)	8 yd (7 m)
Kitchen						
6′ × 10′ (1.8 × 3.0 m)	7 sq yd (6 sq m)	8 sq yd (7 sq m)	3 sq yd (3 sq m)	4 sq yd (4 sq m)	3 yd (3 m)	14 yd (13 m)
6′ × 12′ (1.8 × 3.6 m)	8 sq yd (7 sq m)	12 sq yd (10 sq m)	3 sq yd (3 sq m)	4 sq yd (4 sq m)	4 yd (4 m)	14 yd (13 m)
8′ × 10′ (2.4 × 3.0 m)	9 sq yd (7 sq m)	12 sq yd (10 sq m)	3 sq yd (3 sq m)	4 sq yd (4 sq m)	4 yd (4 m)	14 yd (13 m)
8′ × 12′ (2.4 × 3.6 m)	11 sq yd (9 sq m)	13 sq yd (11 sq m)	3 sq yd (3 sq m)	4 sq yd (4 sq m)	6 yd (5 m)	14 yd (13 m)
10′ × 10′ (3.0 × 3.0 m)	11 sq yd (9 sq m)	13 sq yd (11 sq m)	3 sq yd (3 sq m)	4 sq yd (4 sq m)	6 yd (5 m)	14 yd (13 m)
10′ × 12′ (3.0 × 3.6 m)	13 sq yd (11 sq m)	13 sq yd (11 sq m)	3 sq yd (3 sq m)	4 sq yd (4 sq m)	7 yd (6 m)	14 yd (13 m)
10′ × 14′ (3.0 × 4.2 m)	16 sq yd (13 sq m)	13 sq yd (11 sq m)	3 sq yd (3 sq m)	4 sq yd (4 sq m)	7 yd (6 m)	14 yd (13 m)
12′ × 12′ (3.6 × 3.6 m)	16 sq yd (13 sq m)	16 sq yd (13 sq m)	3 sq yd (3 sq m)	4 sq yd (4 sq m)	7 yd (6 m)	14 yd (13 m)
12′ × 14′ (3.6 × 4.2 m)	19 sq yd (15 sq m)	18 sq yd (15 sq m)	3 sq yd (3 sq m)	4 sq yd (4 sq m)	8 yd (7 m)	14 yd (13 m)
W.C.						
3′6″ × 5′ (1.0 × 1.5 m)	2 sq yd (2 sq m)	10 sq yd (8 sq m)	1 sq yd (1 sq m)	2 sq yd (2 sq m)	4 yd (4 m)	7 yd (6 m)
4′ × 5′ (1.2 × 1.5 m)	2 sq yd (2 sq m)	11 sq yd (9 sq m)	1 sq yd (1 sq m)	2 sq yd (2 sq m)	4 yd (4 m)	7 yd (6 m)
4′ × 6′ (1.2 × 1.8 m)	3 sq yd (2 sq m)	12 sq yd (10 sq m)	1 sq yd (1 sq m)	2 sq yd (2 sq m)	6 yd (5 m)	7 yd (6 m)
4′4″ × 5′ (1.3 × 1.5 m)	2 sq yd (2 sq m)	11 sq yd (9 sq m)	1 sq yd (1 sq m)	2 sq yd (2 sq m)	6 yd (5 m)	7 yd (6 m)
4′4″ × 6′ (1.3 × 1.8 m)	3 sq yd (2 sq m)	12 sq yd (10 sq m)	1 sq yd (1 sq m)	2 sq yd (2 sq m)	6 yd (5 m)	7 yd (6 m)
Bathroom						
6′ × 8′ (1.8 × 2.4 m)	5 sq yd (4 sq m)	28 sq yd (23 sq m)	1 sq yd (1 sq m)	7 sq yd (6 sq m)	10 yd (9 m)	15 yd (14 m)
6′ × 10′ (1.8 × 3.0 m)	7 sq yd (5 sq m)	30 sq yd (25 sq m)	1 sq yd (1 sq m)	7 sq yd (6 sq m)	12 yd (11 m)	15 yd (14 m)
7′ × 8′ (2.1 × 2.4 m)	6 sq yd (5 sq m)	28 sq yd (23 sq m)	1 sq yd (1 sq m)	7 sq yd (6 sq m)	11 yd (10 m)	15 yd (14 m)

	Ceiling	Walls	Window	Door	Skirting	Frames
8′ × 8′ (2.4 × 2.4 m)	7 sq yd (6 sq m)	30 sq yd (25 sq m)	1 sq yd (1 sq m)	7 sq yd (6 sq m)	11 yd (10 m)	15 yd (14 m)
8′ × 10′ (2.4 × 3.0 m)	9 sq yd (7 sq m)	34 sq yd (28 sq m)	1 sq yd (1 sq m)	7 sq yd (6 sq m)	12 yd (11 m)	15 yd (14 m)
8′ × 12′ (2.4 × 3.6 m)	11 sq yd (9 sq m)	36 sq yd (30 sq m)	1 sq yd (1 sq m)	7 sq yd (6 sq m)	14 yd (13 m)	15 yd (14 m)

The rates and hours listed in Table 1 should then be applied to the relevant entry in Table 2 to produce the facts necessary to compare the cost of doing the work yourself or employing a painter.

Don't forget, these prices may need adjustment depending on where you live.
Regional adjustments are provided on the inside cover, and further explanation is given in the Preface.

Example 1

Let us assume that you wish to redecorate your dining room size 14′ × 12′ (4.2 × 3.6 metres). The work consists of:

(*a*) scrape off the wallpaper and hanging new paper (basic price £4.50 per roll);
(*b*) one undercoat and one gloss coat to all woodwork;
(*c*) two coats emulsion paint to the ceiling.

You should then apply the hours and prices in Table 1 to the dimensions in Table 2 as follows:

Scrape off one layer of paper from walls	35 sq yd (29 sq m)	15:00 (14:50)	–	1	43.75 (40.60)
Apply standard patterned wallpaper (basic price £4.50 per roll) to walls	35 sq yd (29 sq m)	11:40 (12:05)	31.50 (30.74)	6	80.50 (81.20)
One undercoat and one coat gloss on					
window	3 sq yd (3 sq m)	2:00 (2:10)	1.80 (1.98)	5	11.55 (13.05)
door	4 sq yd (4 sq m)	2:40 (3:00)	2.40 (2.64)	5	15.40 (17.40)
skirting not exceeding 6″ (150 mm) girth	17 yd (15 m)	1:08 (1:42)	2.04 (2.10)	5	26.35 (26.25)
frames 6″–12″ (150–300 mm) girth	16 yd (13 m)	2:40 (3:12)	3.84 (3.64)	5	32.80 (29.25)
Two coats emulsion paint to ceiling	19 sq yd (15 sq m)	4:56 (4:20)	5.70 (5.40)	5	45.60 (39.00)
		40:04 (42:19)	£47.28 (£46.50)		£255.95 (£245.75)

This shows that it should take you about 40 hours to redecorate your living room and the cost of the materials is approximately £50. Alternatively the cost of employing a contractor would be about £250. Note that the difference between the imperial and metric sizes and the effect of rounding off small quantities causes variations in prices and hours.

Example 2

In this example we will assume that you wish to redecorate your bathroom size 8′ × 10′ (2.4 × 3 metres) The work consists of:

(*a*) one undercoat and one gloss coat to all woodwork;
(*b*) two coats emulsion paint to ceiling and approximately half the wall area;
(*c*) scrape off one layer of paper to approximately half the wall area;
(*d*) hang vinyl surface paper (basic price £5.50 per roll) to approximately half the wall area.

The hours and costs for the individual items are set out in Table 1 and the quantities are in Table 2. Notice that the area of 28 square metres for the walls has been divided into two equal parts of 14 square metres for part wall papering and part painting.

Scrape off one layer of paper from walls	17 sq yd (14 sq m)	7:08 (7:00)	–	1	21.25 (19.60)
Vinyl surfaced wallpaper (basic price £5.50 per roll) to walls	17 sq yd (14 sq m)	5:40 (5:50)	18.70 (18.20)	6	39.10 (39.20)
One undercoat and one coat gloss on					
window	1 sq yd (1 sq m)	0:40 (0:44)	0.60 (0.66)	5	3.85 (4.25)
door	6 sq yd (6 sq m)	3:00 (4:24)	3.60 (3.96)	5	23.10 (25.50)
skirting not exceeding 6″ (150 mm) girth	12 yd (11 m)	0:48 (1:06)	1.44 (1.54)	4	18.60 (19.25)
frames 6″–12″ (150–300 mm) girth	15 yd (14 m)	2:30 (2:48)	3.60 (3.92)	5	30.75 (31.50)
Two coats emulsion paint on					
walls	17 sq yd (14 sq m)	5:40 (5:36)	5.10 (5.04)	5	32.30 (29.40)
ceiling	9 sq yd (7 sq m)	3:36 (3:16)	2.70 (2.52)	5	21.60 (18.20)
		29:02 (30:44)	£35.74 (£35.84)		£190.55 (£186.90)

These figures demonstrate that it should take you about 30 hours to complete the work with a material cost of about £35. A contractor would probably charge about £190 for carrying out the same work.

External painting

Painting outside can be a real pleasure when the sun is shining but a nightmare if it is cold and windy, particularly if rain is threatening! All the information given here is based upon the work being done at ground level. 20% to 30% should be added for working from a ladder.

Wash down previously painted surfaces and rub down, width					
over 12″ (300 mm)	1 sq yd	0:20	–	2	1.50
	(1 sq m)	(0:22)	–		(1.65)
6″–12″ (150–300 mm)	1 yd	0:08	–	2	0.50
	(1 m)	(0:09)	–		(0.55)
not exceeding 6″	1 yd	0:03	–	2	0.20
(150 mm)	(1 m)	(0:04)			(0.22)
Burn off existing paint from general surfaces, width					
over 12″ (300 mm)	1 sq yd	1:15	–	3	6.50
	(1 sq m)	(1:20)	–		(6.75)
6″–12″ (150–300 mm)	1 yd	0:30	–	3	1.40
	(1 m)	(0:35)	–		(1.80)
not exceeding 6″	1 yd	0:20	–	3	1.50
(150 mm)	(1 m)	(0:22)			(1.65)
One coat oil based undercoat on general surfaces, width					
over 12″ (300 mm)	1 sq yd	0:25	0.30	5	2.40
	(1 sq m)	(0:28)	(0.33)		(2.60)
6″–12″ (150–300 mm)	1 yd	0:07	0.12	5	1.10
	(1 m)	(0:09)	(0.14)		(1.20)
not exceeding 6″	1 yd	0:03	0.06	5	0.80
(150 mm)	(1 m)	(0:04)	(0.07)		(0.90)

Don't forget, these prices may need adjustment depending on where you live.
Regional adjustments are provided on the inside cover, and further explanation is given in the Preface.

One coat oil based gloss on general surfaces, width					
over 12″ (300 mm)	1 sq yd	0:25	0.30	5	2.40
	(1 sq m)	(0:28)	(0.33)		(2.60)
6″–12″ (150–300 mm)	1 yd	0:07	0.12	5	1.10
	(1 m)	(0:09)	(0.14)		(1.20)
not exceeding 6″	1 yd	0:03	0.06	5	0.80
(150 mm)	(1 m)	(0:04)	(0.07)		(0.90)
Two coats 'Solignum' green preservative on wood					
wrought timber	1 sq yd	0:20	0.25	4	2.50
	(1 sq m)	(0:25)	(0.30)		(2.75)
sawn timber	1 sq yd	0:22	0.30	4	2.70
	(1 sq m)	(0:28)	(0.35)		(3.00)
Two coats 'Cuprinol' green preservative on wood					
wrought (smooth) timber	1 sq yd	0:22	0.65	4	3.00
	(1 sq m)	(0:28)	(0.80)		(3.30)
sawn (rough) timber	1 sq yd	0:25	0.75	4	3.20
	(1 sq m)	(0:30)	(0.90)		(3.50)
Two coats 'Cuprinol' wood preservative on wood					
wrought (smooth) timber	1 sq yd	0:22	0.70	5	3.10
	(1 sq m)	(0:28)	(0.85)		(3.40)
sawn (rough) timber	1 sq yd	0:25	0.80	5	3.30
	(1 sq m)	(0:30)	(0.95)		(3.60)
Two coats creosote on wood					
wrought timber	1 sq yd	0:30	0.25	5	2.50
	(1 sq m)	(0:35)	(0.30)		(2.75)
sawn timber	1 sq yd	0:35	0.28	5	2.65
	(1 sq m)	(0:40)	(0.33)		(2.90)
One coat 'Blue Circle' stabilising solution and one coat 'Snowcem' finish on					
brickwork	1 sq yd	0:40	0.55	5	2.50
	(1 sq m)	(0:45)	(0.65)		(2.75)
concrete	1 sq yd	0:40	0.60	5	2.60
	(1 sq m)	(0:45)	(0.70)		(2.85)
cement rendering	1 sq yd	0:35	0.60	5	2.50
	(1 sq m)	(0:40)	(0.70)		(2.75,
rough cast	1 sq yd	0:45	1.20	5	3.20
	(1 sq m)	(0:50)	(1.50)		(3.50)

One coat 'Blue Circle' stabilising solution and one coat 'Sandtex Matt' finish on

brickwork	1 sq yd	0:40	0.90	5	2.70
	(1 sq m)	(0:45)	(1.10)		(3.00)
concrete	1 sq yd	0:40	0.80	5	2.80
	(1 sq m)	(0:45)	(1.00)		(3.10)
cement rendering	1 sq yd	0:35	0.90	5	2.75
	(1 sq m)	(0:40)	(1.10)		(3.00)
rough cast	1 sq yd	0:45	1.30	5	3.35
	(1 sq m)	(0:50)	(1.60)		(3.70)

Don't forget, these prices may need adjustment depending on where you live.
Regional adjustments are provided on the inside cover, and further explanation is given in the Preface.

Home security

Making your home safe from fire and burglary is vital but the installation of the equipment is probably better left in the hands of the expert. The following prices are based upon information supplied by Channel Safety Systems Ltd and should be regarded as indicative.

Fire alarms

Self contained smoke detector complete with battery and alarm cable	£35 each

Intruder alarm system

The following prices relate to the installation of the equipment only excluding the cable. The cost of laying 4 core cable could be estimated at approximately 50p per metre which should be added to the following prices.

Single zone panel size 229 × 152 × 76 mm	£125 each
Two tone panel to BS 4737	£200 each
12 Volt internal alarm siren	£30 each
Weatherproof self-activating bell and red housing	£80 each
Recessed or surface magnetic door proximity switch	£15 each
Stair pressure mat	£9 each
Floor pressure mat	£12 each
Panic button	£12 each
Vibration window contact	£25 each
Infra red detector 12 metre range	£75 each
Door connector loops	£8 each
Self contained ultrasonic space alarm	£175 each

Paths and edgings

The figures quoted in this section are based upon unit rates, i.e. prices and hours per square yard or metre and it is assumed that the area to be laid is between 5 and 40 square yards. The unit cost for smaller areas would be more expensive but would be cheaper (per square yard or metre) for areas over 40 square yards. It is assumed that you will do the excavation by hand and the surplus excavated material will be wheeled to a skip (situated within 30 yards of the working area) which will be filled.

You will notice that in some of the build-ups for the unit prices, only the total price has been entered in the Contractor's price column because a contractor would probably calculate his costs on an overall or job basis rather than on an elevation of individual items.

Paths

Precast concrete flagged paths

Preparatory work					
Excavate 6″ deep (150 mm) by hand to remove soil and load into skip	1 sq yd (1 sq m)	0:40 (0:45)	–	2	
Remove from site by skip	0.2 cu yd (0.15 cu m)	–	0.75 (0.85)	–	
4″ thick (100 mm) bed of sand	1 sq yd (1 sq m)	0:20 (0:22)	0.55 (0.60)	2	
per square yard		1:00	£1.30		£3.80
per square metre		(1:07)	(£1.45)		(£4.20)

These costs should be added to the following figures for different finishes to arrive at a composite square yard rate.

2″ (50 mm) thick precast concrete natural colour flags size					
1′6″ × 1′6″ (450 × 450 mm)	1 sq yd (1 sq m)	0:40 (0:45)	6.80 (7.50)	5	12.00 (13.20)
2′0″ × 1′6″ (600 × 450 mm)	1 sq yd (1 sq m)	0:35 (0:40)	6.35 (7.00)	5	11.50 (12.60)

2′0″ × 2′0″ (600 × 600 mm)	1 sq yd	0:30	5.90	5	11.00
	(1 sq m)	(0:35)	(6.50)		(12.10)
2′0″ × 3′0″ (600 × 900 mm)	1 sq yd	0:25	5.00	5	10.00
	(1 sq m)	(0:30)	(5.50)		(11.00)
2″ (50 mm) thick precast concrete coloured flags size					
1′6″ × 1′6″ (450 × 450 mm)	1 sq yd	0:40	10.00	5	15.00
	(1 sq m)	(0:45)	(11.00)		(16.50)
2′0″ × 1′6″ (600 × 450 mm)	1 sq yd	0:35	9.50	5	14.00
	(1 sq m)	(0:40)	(10.50)		(15.40)
2′0″ × 2′0″ (600 × 600 mm)	1 sq yd	0:30	8.60	5	13.00
	(1 sq m)	(0:35)	(9.50)		(14.30)
2′0″ × 3′0″ (600 × 900 mm)	1 sq yd	0:25	7.30	5	12.00
	(1 sq m)	(0:30)	(8.00)		(13.20)
Marshalls concrete keyblok 2½″ (65 mm) thick					
grey	1 sq yd	1:00	6.50	5	14.00
	(1 sq m)	(1:05)	(7.10)		(15.40)
coloured	1 sq yd	1:00	7.00	5	15.00
	(1 sq m)	(1:05)	(7.70)		(16.50)
red	1 sq yd	1:00	7.20	5	15.20
	(1 sq m)	(1:05)	(7.90)		(16.70)
brindle	1 sq yd	1:00	7.50	5	15.50
	(1 sq m)	(1:05)	(8.25)		(17.00)
Marshalls concrete keyblok 3″ (80 mm) thick					
grey	1 sq yd	1:10	7.50	5	15.50
	(1 sq m)	(1:15)	(8.25)		(17.00)
coloured	1 sq yd	1:10	8.20	5	16.50
	(1 sq m)	(1:15)	(9.00)		(18.00)
red	1 sq yd	1:10	8.50	5	16.70
	(1 sq m)	(1:15)	(9.30)		(18.20)
brindle	1 sq yd	1:10	8.80	5	17.00
	(1 sq m)	(1:15)	(9.70)		(18.70)
Marshalls concrete monoblok 2½″ (65 mm) thick					
grey	1 sq yd	1:00	7.00	5	14.40
	(1 sq m)	(1:05)	(7.70)		(16.00)
coloured	1 sq yd	1:00	8.00	5	15.50
	(1 sq m)	(1:05)	(8.80)		(17.00)
red	1 sq yd	1:00	8.10	5	15.70
	(1 sq m)	(1:05)	(8.90)		(17.20)

Marshalls concrete monoblok 3″ (80 mm) thick					
grey	1 sq yd	1:10	7.50	5	16.00
	(1 sq m)	(1:15)	(8.25)		(17.60)
coloured	1 sq yd	1:10	9.00	5	17.20
	(1 sq m)	(1:15)	(9.90)		(19.00)
red	1 sq yd	1:10	9.20	5	17.30
	(1 sq m)	(1:15)	(10.20)		(19.20)

In situ concrete paths (1:2:4 cement, sand and aggregate)

Excavate 8″ (200 mm) deep by hand to remove soil and load into skip	1 sq yd (1 sq m)	0:50 (0:55)	–	2	
Remove from site by skip	0.27 cu yd (0.2 cu m)	–	0.90 (1.00)	–	
4″ thick (100 mm) bed of hardcore blinded with sand	1 sq yd (1 sq m)	1:05 (1:15)	0.90 (1.00)	2	
4″ thick (100 mm) bed of concrete trowelled smooth	1 sq yd (1 sq m)	1:00 (1:10)	4.80 (5.30)	4	
Formwork and supports to edge of path 4″ high (100 mm)	2 yd (2 m)	1:35 (1:50)	2.50 (2.80)	4	
per square yard		4:30	£9.10		£17.50
per square metre		(5:10)	(£10.10)		(£19.25)

In this example it has been assumed that the concrete will be delivered ready mixed and the hours represent the time it will take you to barrow the concrete a distance not exceeding 30 yards including placing and trowelling.

Don't forget, these prices may need adjustment depending on where you live.
Regional adjustments are provided on the inside cover, and further explanation is given in the Preface.

Edgings

Quite often a surface area is bounded by a pin kerb or brick edging which both delineates a boundary and forms a pleasing feature. Costings are presented below and it is assumed that the concrete required for the beds and backings will be ready mixed delivered within 30 yards of the place of work and that the small amount of surplus excavated material will be disposed of in the garden area.

Precast concrete

Excavate shallow trench size 12″ × 6″ deep (300 × 150 mm)	1 yd (1 m)	0:10 (0:12)	–	2	
Concrete (1:3:6 cement, sand, aggregate) in bed and backing to kerb	1 yd (1 m)	0:20 (0:22)	2.60 (2.85)	2	
6″ × 2″ (150 × 50 mm) precast concrete pin kerb	1 yd (1 m)	0:40 (0:45)	2.50 (2.75)	5	
per linear yard		1:10	£5.10		£7.50
per linear metre		(1:19)	(£5.60)		(£8.25)

Brick edgings

Excavate shallow trench size 9″ × 4″ deep (225 × 100 mm)	1 yd (1 m)	0:10 (0:12)	–	2	
Brick-on-edge facing brick bedded, jointed and pointed in cement mortar	1 yd (1 m)	1:00 (1:05)	4.00 (4.40)	5	
per linear yard		1:10	£4.00		£6.00
per linear metre		(1:17)	(£4.40)		(£6.60)

Fencing

You have a wide choice of fencing that can be used to mark house boundaries and the erection should be within the range of skills of the average DIY enthusiast. All the fencing quoted is given per linear yard (linear metres in brackets) and assumes that post holes (where applicable) have been dug by hand and that concrete is ready mixed deposited within 30 yards of the place of working.

Existing work					
Remove fencing and posts					
Chainlink fencing, height					
1200 mm	1 yd (1 m)	0:20 (0:22)	–	2	1.75 (1.90)
1800 mm	1 yd (1 m)	0:30 (0:35)	–	2	2.25 (2.50)
Close boarded timber fencing, height					
1200 mm	1 yd (1 m)	0:35 (0:40)	–	2	3.50 (3.85)
1800 mm	1 yd (1 m)	0:45 (0:50)	–	2	4.00 (4.40)
Chestnut pale wired fencing, height					
900 mm	1 yd (1 m)	0:15 (0:18)	–	2	1.50 (1.65)
1200 mm	1 yd (1 m)	0:20 (0:22)	–	2	2.00 (2.20)
New work					
Three line wire fencing 3′6″ high (1050 mm) on pointed timber posts driven into the ground	1 yd (1 m)	0:45 (0:50)	2.15 (2.35)	4	3.80 (4.20)
Chestnut pale fencing 3′0″ high (900 mm) on two lines of wire fixed to pointed timber posts driven into the ground	1 yd (1 m)	0:30 (0:35)	4.25 (4.70)	4	8.00 (8.80)
As above but 4′0″ high (1200 mm)	1 yd (1 m)	0:40 (0:45)	5.80 (6.40)	5	10.00 (11.00)

Timber close boarded fence 3′6″ high (1050 mm) on two horizontal rails and timber posts set in concrete	1 yd (1 m)	2:00 (2:20)	11.85 (12.50)	6	19.00 (21.00)
As above but 5′6″ high (1650 mm)	1 yd (1 m)	3:40 (4:00)	14.60 (16.00)	6	23.50 (25.80)
Interwoven panel fencing 3′0″ high (900 mm) fixed to timber posts set in concrete	1 yd (1 m)	1:20 (1:30)	9.25 (10.20)	5	18.00 (19.80)
As above but 5′0″ high (1500 mm)	1 yd (1 m)	2:25 (2:40)	11.60 (12.75)	5	20.00 (22.00)
Galvanised chainlink fencing 3′0″ high (900 mm) on concrete posts set in concrete	1 yd (1 m)	1:25 (1:35)	5.60 (6.15)	5	10.00 (11.00)
As above but 5′0″ high (1500 mm)	1 yd (1 m)	1:55 (2:05)	8.20 (9.00)	5	12.50 (13.75)
Plastic coated chain link fencing 3′0″ high (900 mm) on concrete posts set in concrete	1 yd (1 m)	1:25 (1:35)	6.00 (6.60)	5	11.00 (12.20)
As above but 5′0″ high (1500 mm)	1 yd (1 m)	1:55 (2:05)	9.00 (9.90)	5	13.80 (14.30)

Don't forget, these prices may need adjustment depending on where you live.

Regional adjustments are provided on the inside cover, and further explanation is given in the Preface.

Patios

Laying a patio can add a very attractive feature to your house. You can use a wide variety of materials and a selection of them have been included in the costings set out below. It is assumed that all the excavated material will be barrowed to a skip placed within 30 yards of the patio.

The information set out in 'Paths and edgings' has been used to provide the overall costs of the following size patios and the figures include the preparatory work. Please note that the examples assume that the skip or mini skip will be filled so some distortion in costs may occur in the calculation of small areas.

Patio size 12′ × 9′ (3.66 × 2.75 m)

2″ (50 mm) thick precast concrete natural colour flags, size					
1′6″ × 1′6″ (450 × 450 mm)	12 sq yd (10 sq m)	20:00 (18:40)	97.20 (90.40)	5	189.60 (174.00)
2′0″ × 1′6″ (600 × 450 mm)	12 sq yd (10 sq m)	19:00 (17:50)	91.80 (84.50)	5	183.60 (168.00)
2′0″ × 2′0″ (600 × 600 mm)	12 sq yd (10 sq m)	18:00 (17:00)	86.40 (79.50)	5	177.60 (163.00)
2′0″ × 3′0″ (600 × 900 mm)	12 sq yd (10 sq m)	17:00 (16:10)	75.60 (69.50)	5	165.60 (152.00)
2″ (50 mm) thick precast concrete coloured flags, size					
1′6″ × 1′6″ (450 × 450 mm)	12 sq yd (10 sq m)	20:00 (18:40)	135.60 (124.50)	5	225.60 (207.00)
2′0″ × 1′6″ (600 × 450 mm)	12 sq yd (10 sq m)	19:00 (17:50)	129.60 (119.50)	5	213.60 (196.00)
2′0″ × 2′0″ (600 × 600 mm)	12 sq yd (10 sq m)	18:00 (17:00)	118.80 (109.50)	5	201.60 (185.00)
2′0″ × 3′0″ (600 × 900 mm)	12 sq yd (10 sq m)	17:00 (16:10)	103.20 (94.50)	5	189.60 (174.00)

Marshalls concrete keyblok 2½" (65 mm) thick					
grey	12 sq yd (10 sq m)	24:00 (22:00)	93.60 (85.50)	5	213.60 (196.00)
coloured	12 sq yd (10 sq m)	24:00 (22:00)	99.60 (91.50)	5	225.60 (207.00)
red	12 sq yd (10 sq m)	24:00 (22:00)	100.00 (93.50)	5	228.00 (209.00)
brindle	12 sq yd (10 sq m)	24:00 (22:00)	105.60 (97.00)	5	231.60 (212.00)
Marshalls concrete keyblok 3" (80 mm) thick					
grey	12 sq yd (10 sq m)	26:00 (23:40)	105.60 (97.00)	5	231.60 (212.00)
coloured	12 sq yd (10 sq m)	26:00 (23:40)	114.00 (104.50)	5	243.60 (222.00)
red	12 sq yd (10 sq m)	26:00 (23:40)	117.60 (107.50)	5	246.00 (224.00)
brindle	12 sq yd (10 sq m)	26:00 (23:40)	121.20 (111.50)	5	249.60 (229.00)

Marshalls concrete monoblok 2½″ (65 mm) thick					
grey	12 sq yd	24:00	99.60	5	219.60
	(10 sq m)	(22:00)	(91.50)		(202.00)
coloured	12 sq yd	24:00	111.60	5	231.60
	(10 sq m)	(22:00)	(102.50)		(212.00)
red	12 sq yd	24:00	112.80	5	234.00
	(10 sq m)	(22:00)	(103.50)		(214.00)
Marshalls concrete monoblok 3″ (80 mm) thick					
grey	12 sq yd	26:00	105.60	5	237.60
	(10 sq m)	(23:40)	(97.00)		(218.00)
coloured	12 sq yd	26:00	123.60	5	252.00
	(10 sq m)	(23:40)	(113.50)		(232.00)
red	12 sq yd	26:00	126.00	5	253.20
	(10 sq m)	(23:40)	(116.50)		(234.00)

Patio size 24′ × 9′ (7.32 × 2.75 m)

2″ (50 mm) thick precast concrete natural colour flags, size					
1′6″ × 1′6″ (450 × 450 mm)	24 sq yd	40:00	194.40	5	379.20
	(20 sq m)	(37:20)	(179.00)		(348.00)
2′0″ × 1′6″ (600 × 450 mm)	24 sq yd	38:00	184.00	5	367.20
	(20 sq m)	(35:40)	(169.00)		(336.00)
2′0″ × 2′0″ (600 × 600 mm)	24 sq yd	36:00	172.80	5	355.20
	(20 sq m)	(34:00)	(159.00)		(326.00)
2′0″ × 3′0″ (600 × 900 mm)	24 sq yd	34:00	151.20	5	331.20
	(20 sq m)	(32:20)	(139.00)		(304.00)

Don't forget, these prices may need adjustment depending on where you live.

Regional adjustments are provided on the inside cover, and further explanation is given in the Preface.

2″ (50 mm) thick precast concrete coloured flags, size					
1′6″ × 1′6″ (450 × 450 mm)	24 sq yd	40:00	271.20	5	451.20
	(20 sq m)	(37:20)	(249.00)		(414.00)
2′0″ × 1′6″ (600 × 450 mm)	24 sq yd	38:00	259.00	5	427.20
	(20 sq m)	(35:40)	(239.00)		(392.00)
2′0″ × 2′0″ (600 × 600 mm)	24 sq yd	36:00	231.60	5	403.20
	(20 sq m)	(34:00)	(219.00)		(370.00)
2′0″ × 3′0″ (600 × 900 mm)	24 sq yd	34:00	206.40	5	379.20
	(20 sq m)	(32:20)	(189.00)		(348.00)
Marshalls concrete keyblok 2½″ (65 mm) thick					
grey	24 sq yd	48:00	187.20	5	427.20
	(20 sq m)	(44:00)	(171.00)		(392.00)
coloured	24 sq yd	48:00	199.20	5	451.20
	(20 sq m)	(44:00)	(183.00)		(414.00)
red	24 sq yd	48:00	204.00	5	456.00
	(20 sq m)	(44:00)	(187.00)		(418.00)
brindle	24 sq yd	48:00	211.20	5	463.20
	(20 sq m)	(44:00)	(184.00)		(424.00)
Marshalls concrete keyblok 3″ (80 mm) thick					
grey	24 sq yd	52:00	211.20	5	463.20
	(20 sq m)	(47:20)	(184.00)		(424.00)
coloured	24 sq yd	52:00	228.00	5	487.20
	(20 sq m)	(47:20)	(209.05)		(444.00)
red	24 sq yd	52:00	235.20	5	492.00
	(20 sq m)	(47:20)	(215.00)		(448.00)
brindle	24 sq yd	52:00	242.40	5	499.20
	(20 sq m)	(47:00)	(223.00)		(458.00)
Marshalls concrete monoblok 2½″ (65 mm) thick					
grey	24 sq yd	48:00	199.20	5	439.20
	(20 sq m)	(44:00)	(183.00)		(404.00)
coloured	24 sq yd	48:00	223.20	5	463.20
	(20 sq m)	(44:00)	(205.00)		(424.00)
red	24 sq yd	48:00	226.60	5	468.00
	(20 sq m)	(44:00)	(207.00)		(428.00)

Marshalls concrete monoblok 3″ (80 mm) thick					
grey	24 sq yd (20 sq m)	52:00 (47:20)	211.20 (194.00)	5	475.20 (436.00)
coloured	24 sq yd (20 sq m)	52:00 (47:20)	247.20 (227.00)	5	503.20 (464.00)
red	24 sq yd (20 sq m)	52:00 (47:20)	252.00 (229.00)	5	507.40 (468.00)

Patio size 30′ × 15′ (9.15 × 4.57 m)

2″ (50 mm) thick precast concrete natural colour flags, size					
1′6″ × 1′6″ (450 × 450 mm)	50 sq yd (42 sq m)	63:20 (59:44)	405.00 (375.90)	5	790.00 (730.80)
2′0″ × 1′6″ (600 × 450 mm)	50 sq yd (42 sq m)	59:10 (56.14)	382.50 (354.90)	5	765.00 (705.60)
2′0″ × 2′0″ (600 × 600 mm)	50 sq yd (42 sq m)	55:00 (52.44)	360.00 (333.90)	5	740.00 (684.60)
2′0″ × 3′0″ (600 × 900 mm)	50 sq yd (42 sq m)	50:50 (49:14)	315.00 (291.90)	5	690.00 (638.40)
2″ (50 mm) thick precast concrete coloured flags, size					
1′6″ × 1′6″ (450 × 450 mm)	50 sq yd (42 sq m)	63:20 (59:44)	565.00 (522.90)	5	940.00 (869.40)
2′0″ × 1′6″ (600 × 450 mm)	50 sq yd (42 sq m)	59:10 (56.14)	540.00 (501.90)	5	890.00 (823.20)
2′0″ × 2′0″ (600 × 600 mm)	50 sq yd (42 sq m)	55:00 (52.44)	495.00 (459.90)	5	840.00 (777.00)
2′0″ × 3′0″ (600 × 900 mm)	50 sq yd (42 sq m)	50:50 (49:14)	430.00 (396.90)	5	790.00 (730.80)

Don't forget, these prices may need adjustment depending on where you live.
Regional adjustments are provided on the inside cover, and further explanation is given in the Preface.

Marshalls concrete keyblok 2½" (65 mm) thick					
grey	50 sq yd	80:00	390.00	5	890.00
	(42 sq m)	(73:44)	(354.90)		(823.20)
coloured	50 sq yd	80:00	415.00	5	940.00
	(42 sq m)	(73:44)	(384.30)		(869.40)
red	50 sq yd	80:00	425.00	5	950.00
	(42 sq m)	(73:44)	(392.70)		(877.80)
brindle	50 sq yd	80:00	440.00	5	965.00
	(42 sq m)	(73:44)	(407.40)		(890.40)
Marshalls concrete keyblok 3" (80 mm) thick					
grey	50 sq yd	88:20	440.00	5	965.00
	(42 sq m)	(80:44)	(407.40)		(890.40)
coloured	50 sq yd	88:20	475.00	5	1015.00
	(42 sq m)	(80:44)	(438.90)		(932.40)
red	50 sq yd	88:20	490.00	5	1025.00
	(42 sq m)	(80:44)	(451.50)		(940.80)
brindle	50 sq yd	88:20	505.00	5	1040.00
	(42 sq m)	(80:44)	(468.30)		(961.80)
Marshalls concrete monoblok 2½" (65 mm) thick					
grey	50 sq yd	80:00	415.00	5	915.00
	(42 sq m)	(73:44)	(384.30)		(848.40)
coloured	50 sq yd	80:00	465.00	5	965.00
	(42 sq m)	(73:44)	(430.50)		(890.40)
red	50 sq yd	80:00	470.00	5	975.00
	(42 sq m)	(73:44)	(434.70)		(898.80)
Marshalls concrete monoblok 3" (80 mm) thick					
grey	50 sq yd	88:20	440.00	5	990.00
	(42 sq m)	(80:44)	(406.40)		(915.60)
coloured	50 sq yd	88:20	515.00	5	1050.00
	(42 sq m)	(80:44)	(476.20)		(974.40)
red	50 sq yd	88:20	525.00	5	1055.00
	(42 sq m)	(80:44)	(480.90)		(982.80)

Don't forget, these prices may need adjustment depending on where you live.
Regional adjustments are provided on the inside cover, and further explanation is given in the Preface.

Walling

Brick or stone walling constructed in gardens usually acts as a demarcation line between different surfaces and/or levels. The information given in this section generally applies to walls up to 3 feet (approximately 1 metre) high. It is assumed that you will excavate by hand and that the surplus excavated material will be spread and levelled over the garden area and also that concrete is ready mixed and will be deposited within 30 yards of the place of work. The mortar is assumed to be mixed by hand at the point of placing.

The comments at the front of the Paths and edgings section (p.141) on the single entry in the Contractor's price column also apply here.

Preparatory work

Excavate trench size 1′6″ × 9″ deep (450 × 225 mm)	1 yd (1 m)	0:20 (0:25)	–	2	
Concrete (1:3:6 cement, sand, aggregate) in wall foundation	1 yd (1 m)	0:15 (0:20)	3.35 (4.00)	3	
per linear yard per linear metre		0:35 (0:45)	£3.35 (£4.00)		£6.00 (£6.60)

These costs should be added to the following figures for different kinds of walling to arrive at a composite rate per linear yard or metre for walling 1 yard or metre high as shown.

4½″ thick (112 mm wide) brick wall in common bricks (£120 per 1000) in cement mortar overall	1 yd (1 m)	2:00 (2:30)	9.50 (11.00)	6	23.00 (27.50)
Add or *deduct* £0.30 to the Total DIY Material column for every £5.00 variation per 1000 in the price of common bricks	–	–	–	–	–

9″ thick (225 mm wide) brick wall in facing bricks (£275 per 1000) in cement mortar with brick-on-edge coping overall	1 yd (1 m)	3:50 (4:40)	35.80 (38.00)	6	65.00 (75.00)
Add or *deduct* £0.60 to the Total DIY Material column for each £5.00 variation per 1000 in the price of facing bricks	–	–	–	–	–
12″ thick (300 mm) random rubble stone wall (£68.00 per tonne) laid dry with regular coping	1 yd (1 m)	4:20 (5:10)	40.00 (45.00)	8	80.00 (90.00)
Add or *deduct* £2.60 to the Total DIY Material column for each £5.00 variation per tonne in the price of stone	–	–	–	–	–
12″ thick (300 mm) random rubble stone wall (£58.00 per tonne) in cement mortar with level coping	1 yd (1 m)	3:90 (4:40)	47.00 (53.00)	8	75.00 (85.00)
Add or *deduct* £2.60 to the Total DIY Material column for each £5.00 variation per tonne in the price of stone	–	–	–	–	–
4″ thick (100 mm) 'Marshalite' reconstructed stone walling (£85.00 per 100 blocks) in cement mortar	1 yd (1 m)	2:15 (2:40)	38.50 (45.00)	8	54.00 (60.00)
Add or *deduct* £2.40 to the Total DIY Material column for each £5.00 variation per 100 blocks in the price of stone	–	–	–	–	–

Don't forget, these prices may need adjustment depending on where you live.

Regional adjustments are provided on the inside cover, and further explanation is given in the Preface.

Ornamental pools

There are two types of ornamental pools – preformed plastic and those you construct. The plastic type are so diverse in size and shape that it is not possible to include them – visit your local garden centre for the cost and add it to the excavation figures listed below.

You can easily construct an ornamental pool these days thanks to new techniques and materials that are available. Concrete and brickwork are no longer the only choices so the whole job can now be completed much quicker.

When designing your pool, remember to form one deep part so that the fish can survive when the pool is frozen over.

It is assumed that the excavation will be done by hand and the surplus excavated material will be placed in another part of the garden. If it is necessary to hire a skip you should use the costs as set out in 'Disposal of rubbish'.

Excavate and place surplus	1 cu yd	3:00	–	2	18.00
material within 15 yards distance	(1 cu m)	(3:45)			(22.50)
Butyl sheeting					
economy	1 sq yd	0:02	6.80	3	8.20
	(1 sq m)	(0:03)	(8.20)		(9.80)
heavy duty	1 sq yd	0:03	8.75	3	10.20
	(1 sq m)	(0:04)	(10.50)		(12.20)
Coloured PVC sheeting					
standard	1 sq yd	0:02	4.50	3	5.00
	(1 sq m)	(0:03)	(5.40)		(6.00)
heavy duty	1 sq yd	0:03	5.30	3	6.35
	(1 sq m)	(0:04)	(6.35)		(7.50)

SKIP HIRE
DO NOT OVERFILL
MINI-SKIP

5 Hiring plant

The success of carrying out do-it-yourself jobs depends upon having the right tools and equipment. Most householders own standard tools such as hammers, screwdrivers and chisels but there is a wide range of other tools which may only be needed every couple of years or so.

You would be foolish to buy equipment and tools for these occasional needs and the answer lies in hiring them. The following comprehensive list of the plant, tools and equipment for domestic use is based upon information kindly supplied by Hire Service Shops, 23 Willow Lane, Mitcham, Surrey, CR4 4TS who have shops all over the country and the prices include VAT.

	First 24 hrs £	Addit. 24 hrs £	Per week £
Access towers/scaffolding			
Alloy stairway/span tower base size 4′3″ × 5′0″ (1.3 × 1.5 m) or 2′8″ × 5′0″ (0.8 × 1.5 m), height			
8′3″ (2.5 m)	20.13	10.06	40.25
15′0″ (4.5 m)	29.90	14.95	59.80
21′6″ (6.5 m)	39.68	19.84	79.35
28′0″ (8.5 m)	49.45	24.73	98.90
34′6″ (10.5 m)	59.23	29.61	118.45
add for each additional 6′6″ (2 m), height	9.78	4.89	19.55

	First 24 hrs £	Addit. 24 hrs £	Per week £
Alloy wide span tower base size 4′3″ × 8′3″ (1.3 × 2.5 m) or 2′8″ × 8′3″ (0.8 × 2.5 m), height			
8′3″ (2.5 m)	21.28	10.64	42.55
15′0″ (4.5 m)	32.20	16.10	64.40
21′6″ (6.5 m)	43.13	21.56	86.25
28′0″ (8.5 m)	54.05	27.03	108.10
34′6″ (10.5 m)	64.98	32.49	129.95
add for each additional 6′6″ (2 m), height	10.93	5.46	21.85
Alloy chimney scaffold unit			
half chimney surround unit	33.35	16.68	66.70
Steel domestic towers base size 4′3″ × 2′0″ (1.3 × 0.6 m), height			
4′ (1.2 m)	5.75	2.88	11.50
6′ (1.8 m)	7.13	3.57	14.26
8′ (2.4 m)	8.51	4.26	17.02
10′ (3.0 m)	9.89	4.95	19.78
12′ (3.6 m)	11.27	5.64	22.54
14′ (4.2 m)	12.65	6.33	25.30
16′ (4.8 m)	14.03	7.02	28.06
Base size 4′3″ × 4′4″ (1.3 × 1.3 m), height			
4′ (1.2 m)	8.05	4.03	16.10
6′ (1.8 m)	9.43	4.72	18.86
8′ (2.4 m)	10.81	5.41	21.62
10′ (3.0 m)	12.19	6.10	24.38
12′ (3.6 m)	13.57	6.79	27.14
14′ (4.2 m)	14.95	7.48	29.90
16′ (4.8 m)	16.33	8.17	32.66
add for each additional 2′ (0.6 m), height	1.38	0.69	2.76
staircase frame	1.15	0.58	2.30
additional set of bases	–	–	4.60

	First 24 hrs £	Addit. 24 hrs £	Per week £
Steel industrial towers base size 5′ × 7′ (1.5 × 2.1 m), or 7′ × 7′ (2.1 × 2.1 m), height			
8′ (2.4 m)	14.95	7.48	29.90
12′ (3.6 m)	18.40	9.20	36.80
16′ (4.8 m)	21.85	10.93	43.70
20′ (6.0 m)	25.30	12.65	50.60
24′ (7.2 m)	28.75	14.38	57.50
28′ (8.5 m)	32.20	16.10	64.40
32′ (9.8 m)	35.65	17.83	71.30
Steel industrial towers base size 7′ × 10′ (2.1 × 3.0 m), or 10′ × 10′ (3.0 × 3.0 m), height			
8′ (2.4 m)	20.70	10.35	41.40
12′ (3.6 m)	24.15	12.08	48.30
16′ (4.8 m)	27.60	13.80	55.20
20′ (6.0 m)	31.05	15.53	62.10
24′ (7.2 m)	34.50	17.25	69.00
28′ (8.5 m)	37.95	18.98	75.90
32′ (9.8 m)	41.40	20.70	82.80
add for each additional 2′ (0.6 m), height	1.73	0.86	3.45
additional set of bases	–	–	6.90
Ladders/support equipment			
Wood/aluminium ladders, double			
12′ extending to 21′	6.33	3.16	12.65
14′ extending to 25′	7.48	3.74	14.95
16′ extending to 29′	9.20	4.60	18.40
Wood/aluminium ladders, treble			
10′ extending to 26′	8.05	4.03	16.10
12′ extending to 32′	9.78	4.89	19.55
Aluminium ladders, heavy duty, double			
20′ extending to 37′	13.80	6.90	27.60
Aluminium ladders, heavy duty, treble			
16′ extending to 42′	18.98	9.49	37.95
20′ extending to 54′	24.15	12.08	48.30

	First 24 hrs £	Addit. 24 hrs £	Per week £
Roof ladders			
alloy and wooden 14′ and 16′	8.63	4.31	17.25
Ladder stay (each)	3.45	1.73	6.90
Builder's steps,			
8 tread, height 5′6″	4.03	2.01	8.05
10 tread, height 7′8″	5.18	2.59	10.35
12 tread, height 9′10″	5.75	2.88	11.50
Decorator's trestles, height			
6′	4.03	2.01	8.05
8′	5.18	2.59	10.35
10′	5.75	2.88	11.50
12′	6.33	3.16	12.65
14′	6.90	3.45	13.80
Steel splitheads			
nos 1 to 4 – 1′9″ extending to 8′0″	–	–	2.30
Steel trestles			
nos 1 to 4 – 1′9″ extending to 8′0″	–	–	2.88
Steel props			
nos 0 to 4 – 3′6″ extending to 16′0″	–	–	2.30
jackall prop	4.60	2.30	9.20
Lightweight staging, length			
8′	4.03	1.73	8.05
10′	5.18	2.59	10.35
12′	6.33	3.16	12.65
16′	7.48	3.74	14.95
20′	9.20	4.60	18.40
24′	11.50	5.75	23.00
Scaffold boards, length			
8′–10′, 11′–13′	–	–	1.44

Power/lighting/welding

	First 24 hrs £	Addit. 24 hrs £	Per week £
Generators			
KVA Petrol, 110/240 Volt			
1.5 – 2.0	23.58	12.08	47.15
3.0 – 3.5	27.60	13.80	55.20
KVA Diesel, 110/240 Volt			
4.0 – 5.0	33.35	16.68	66.70
8.0 – 10.0	45.43	22.71	90.85
12.5 – 15.0	60.38	30.19	120.75

	First 24 hrs £	Addit. 24 hrs £	Per week £
Transformers			
2.2 KVA	4.03	2.01	8.05
3.0 KVA	5.75	2.88	11.50
4.0 KVA	8.05	4.03	16.10
5.0 KVA	10.35	5.18	20.70
7.5 KVA	12.65	6.33	25.30
10 – 15 KVA	18.40	9.20	36.80
Extension cable			
50′ cable/drum	2.88	1.44	5.75
Fourway junction box	4.60	2.30	9.20
Floodlights			
Gas			
large tripod mounted	5.75	2.88	11.50
small cylinder mounted	4.60	2.30	9.20
Electric			
tripod mounted	7.48	3.74	14.95
Festoon lights industrial	8.05	4.03	16.10
Twin floor 5 m tower mast	11.50	5.75	23.00
Welding			
Site welder, petrol			
20–170 Amp	31.63	15.81	63.25
20–200 Amp	43.70	21.85	87.40
Welder/generator, D. C. diesel			
250 Amp	50.03	25.01	100.05
315 Amp	56.93	28.46	113.85
Arc welder, 204 Volt			
140 Amp/180 Amp	12.08	6.04	24.15
Portapak oxyacetylene welding kit	18.40	9.20	36.80
MIG welder, 240 Volt	12.08	6.04	24.15
Spot welder, 240 Volt (30 Amp)	12.08	6.04	24.15

Concreting equipment

Concrete mixers			
5/3½ cu ft diesel	16.68	9.49	33.35
4/3cu ft (½ bag), petrol	9.78	4.89	19.55
4/3cu ft (½ bag), electric	9.78	4.89	19.55
Concrete finishing			
power finishing trowel, petrol	27.03	13.51	54.05

	First 24 hrs £	Addit. 24 hrs £	Per week £
Poker vibrator			
electric	20.13	10.06	40.25
petrol	23.58	11.79	47.15
diesel	27.03	13.51	54.05
Floor grinder, diesel/electric	36.80	18.40	73.60
Track/floor saw, diesel	41.40	20.70	82.80
Surface scaler/roof dechipper	35.65	17.83	71.30
Needle gun, scaler, air driven	9.78	4.89	19.55
Edge forms	–	–	3.45
Indent roller	4.60	2.30	9.20
Compactors			
Compactor, 2 stroke, petrol	23.58	11.79	47.15
Vibrating plate			
heavy, petrol	27.03	13.51	54.05
medium, petrol	22.43	11.21	44.85
Vibrating roller, diesel/petrol	33.35	16.68	66.70
Cowley site level	9.20	4.60	18.40
Pumping/drain clearing/plumbing			
Water pumps			
Hand operated	6.33	3.16	12.65
Submersible, electric			
1″	8.63	4.31	17.25
2″	18.98	9.49	37.95
Centrifugal, petrol			
2″	23.00	11.50	46.00
3″	25.30	12.65	50.60
Spate 3″ diesel	31.63	15.81	63.25
Additional 20′ delivery hose (all pumps)	–	–	5.75
Drain testing/cleaning tools			
Drain test kit 'U' gauge	3.45	1.73	6.90
Air bag drain stopper	3.45	1.73	6.90
Drain plugs 4″–6″ (per pair)	–	–	3.45
Drain rods and fittings 30′ (per set)	4.60	2.30	9.20
Drain clearing pump	4.60	2.30	9.20
Sink cleaner, hand operated	5.75	2.88	11.50

	First 24 hrs £	Addit. 24 hrs £	Per week £
Drain cleaner, hand operated	8.63	4.31	17.25
Powered drain cleaner, electric	24.15	12.08	48.30
Plumber's tools			
Blowlamp gas – with extension hose	4.60	2.30	9.20
Pipe freezing kit, CO_2	13.80	6.90	27.60
Steel pipe bender 2″, hydraulic	19.55	9.78	39.10
Copper pipe bender (machine only)	9.20	4.60	18.40
Guides and formers, 15–28 mm, 35–42 mm	1.73	0.86	3.45
Steel pipe cutter, up to 2″	3.45	1.73	6.90
Clay pipe cutter, 4″ to 6″	9.20	4.60	18.40
Pipe vice stand	6.90	3.45	13.80
Pipe wrenches			
stillson 12″/18″	–	–	3.45
stillson 24″	3.45	0.86	5.18
stillson 36″	3.45	1.73	6.90
chain 27″	3.45	1.73	6.90
Immersion spanner	–	–	3.45
Pipe threading			
Die stock			
electric	25.30	12.65	50.60
ratchet	8.63	4.31	17.25
Pipe threading machine, electric			
½″–4″	50.03	25.01	100.05
½″–2″	36.80	18.40	73.60
Pipe pressure tester	6.90	3.45	13.80
Building/decorating/fixing			
Damp proof injection unit	21.28	10.64	42.55
Woodwork/dryrot/waterproofing spray unit	21.28	10.64	42.55
Wallpaper steam strippers, gas/electric	11.50	5.75	23.00
Wallpaper perforator	1.73	0.86	3.45
Paint stripper, electric	5.75	2.88	11.50
Stone splitter	21.85	10.93	43.70
Bitumen boiler	14.95	7.48	29.90

	First 24 hrs £	Addit. 24 hrs £	Per week £
Tar furnace	6.33	3.16	12.65
Compound bucket	–	–	3.45
Metal detector	6.90	3.45	13.80
Cable avoiding tool	20.70	10.35	41.40
CAT signal generator	13.80	6.90	27.60
Road hazard equipment			
Traffic warning cones	–	–	1.15
Road warning lamps	–	–	1.15
Flashing lamp and stand, battery	–	–	2.30
Road signs	–	–	3.45
Road barrier, plank and cone	–	–	4.60
Building/decorating tools			
Blowlamp with extension hose	4.60	2.30	9.20
Bolt croppers	3.45	1.73	6.90
Bucket	–	–	1.73
Crowbar	–	–	3.45
Dust sheets	2.30	0.58	3.45
Floorboard cramps	2.30	1.15	4.60
G clamps	–	–	2.30
Paperhanger's table	–	–	3.45
Paving mallet	–	–	4.60
Pickaxe/matlock	–	–	3.45
Punner	–	–	3.45
Sash clamps	–	–	3.45
Shovel/spade	–	–	3.45
Slate ripper	–	–	3.45
Sledgehammer 7/14 lb	–	–	3.45
Spirit level	–	–	3.45
Tarpaulins	4.60	2.30	9.20
Tile cutter	4.60	2.30	9.20
Tile breaker/drill	2.30	1.15	4.60
Tyrolean roughcast machine	4.60	2.30	9.20
Wheelbarrow	3.45	1.73	6.90
Workmate	5.75	2.88	11.50

	4 hrs or 5–9am £	First 24 hrs £	Addit. 24 hrs £	Per week £
Fixing tools				
Cartridge hammer	8.63	11.50	5.75	23.00
Staple tacker, light duty	3.45	4.60	2.30	9.20
Stapling machine, heavy duty	6.33	8.63	4.31	17.25
Impact wrench, air operated	8.63	11.50	5.75	23.00
Impact wrench, electric	6.33	8.63	4.31	17.25
Screwdriver, electric	5.75	7.48	3.74	14.95
Nail gun, air operated	14.38	19.55	9.78	39.10

	First 24 hrs £	Addit. 24 hrs £	Per week £
Heating/cooling/drying			
Industrial heaters, gas			
Plaque heater 9500 BTU	6.33	3.16	12.65
Boxer convector, 80,000 BTU	6.33	3.16	12.65
Forced air, 27–97,000 BTU	15.53	7.76	31.05
Forced air, 30–125,000 BTU	16.68	8.34	33.35
Forced air, 108–250,000 BTU	22.43	11.21	44.85
Industrial heaters, paraffin			
Forced air, 85–100,000 BTU	16.68	8.34	33.35
Forced air, 150,000 BTU	20.13	10.06	40.25
Home/office heaters			
Cabinet, gas 3–16,000 BTU	6.67	3.34	13.34
Electric fan heater, 3 kW	3.22	1.61	6.44
Cooling			
Industrial blower	10.35	5.18	20.70
Air conditioning unit	33.35	16.68	66.70
Drying			
Building dryer, dehumidifier, 30,000 ft^3	31.63	15.81	63.25
Portable building dryer, 5,000 ft^3	23.00	11.50	46.00
Portable fume extracter	28.75	14.38	57.50

	4 hrs or 5–9am £	First 24 hrs £	Addit. 24 hrs £	Per week £
Breaking/drilling				
Hydraulic breaker, petrol/diesel	29.90	40.25	20.13	80.50
Electric hammers				
Heavy breaker, (inc. trolley)	19.55	23.45	13.23	52.90
Demolition hammer	10.93	14.95	7.48	29.90
Light hammer	10.35	13.80	6.90	27.60
Tamping tool	–	–	–	4.60
Comb holder, bush hammer	–	–	–	2.30
Rotary hammers				
Heavy duty, Kango 950/Hilti TE72	10.93	14.95	7.48	29.90
Medium duty, Kango 637/Hilti TE42	10.35	13.80	6.90	27.60
Hammer drills				
Light duty	8.63	11.50	5.75	23.00
Medium duty	9.20	12.65	6.33	25.30
Rotary/hammer drill bits				
Solid drills ½″–1¼″ dia.	–	2.30	1.15	4.60
Core drills ½″–4″ dia.	–	4.60	2.30	9.20
Extension/drive bars	–	–	–	1.73
Electric drills				
Single speed ⅜″ chuck	4.03	5.18	2.59	10.35
Two speed ½″ chuck	5.18	6.90	3.45	13.80
Right angle drill	5.75	7.48	3.74	14.95
Cordless drill	5.18	6.90	3.45	13.80
Four speed drill ¾″–1″ chuck	8.05	10.35	5.18	20.70
Percussion drill ½″–⅛″ chuck	5.75	7.48	3.74	14.95
Masonry drill bits ½″–1″	–	1.73	0.86	3.45
Magnetic base drills				
Magnetic drill stand (drill extra)	13.80	18.40	9.20	36.80
Rotabroach magnetic base drill	19.55	26.45	13.23	52.90

	4 hrs or 5–9am £	First 24 hrs £	Addit. 24 hrs £	Per week £
Saws/saw benches				
Portable saws				
Circular saw 8″/9″ inc. blade	8.05	10.93	5.46	21.85
Jig saw (blades resale only)	7.48	9.78	4.89	19.55
Reciprocating saw (blades resale only)	9.20	12.08	6.04	24.15
Door trimming saw inc. blade	9.20	12.08	6.04	24.15
Metal/masonry saw benches				
Clipper bench saw 14″				
junior, electric	–	31.63	15.81	63.25
major, petrol/electric	–	37.95	18.98	75.90
Table cut off saw 14″, electric	14.38	19.55	9.78	39.10
Tile saw, electric	18.80	25.30	12.65	50.60
Cut off/power saw 12″				
2 stroke, petrol	13.80	18.40	9.20	36.80
electric	13.80	18.40	9.20	36.80
Cut off saw trolley	2.30	3.45	1.73	6.90
Timber saw benches				
Combination saw bench 8″, electric	–	21.85	10.93	43.70
Timber saw bench 12″, electric	–	19.55	9.78	39.10
Combination saw bench 12″, electric	–	35.65	17.83	71.83
Site saw bench 16″, petrol	–	28.75	14.38	57.50
Bench top mitre 'chop saw' 8″, electric	14.38	19.55	9.78	39.10
Floor saw				
Track/floor saw, diesel	–	41.40	20.70	82.80
Chain saws, inc. chain				
18″ 2 stroke, petrol	17.25	23.00	17.25	57.50
18″ electric	13.80	18.00	13.80	46.00
Additional saw chains	–	–	–	9.78

	4 hrs or 5–9am £	First 24 hrs £	Addit. 24 hrs £	Per week £
Cutting/grinding/sanding				
Angle grinders				
Angle grinderette 4″/5″	5.75	7.48	3.74	14.95
Angle grinder				
9″	8.63	11.50	5.75	23.00
12″	13.80	18.40	9.20	36.80
Wall chasing machine				
Chasing machine inc. cutter	15.53	20.70	10.35	41.40
Additional cutters	–	–	–	6.90
Metal cutters				
Metal shears	9.78	13.23	6.61	26.45
Metal nibblers	9.78	13.23	6.61	26.45
Sanders				
Belt sander 4″	8.34	10.93	5.46	21.85
Disc sander 7″	8.05	10.35	5.18	20.70
Orbital sander industrial	8.05	10.35	5.18	20.70
Floor sanders				
Domestic 8″	16.10	21.28	10.64	42.55
Edging sander 7″	12.65	16.68	8.34	33.35
Router	8.63	11.50	5.75	23.00
Power plane	8.63	11.50	5.75	23.00
Spraying/compressors				
Spray units				
Compressor				
2.5 cfm + PS3 gun	23.00	17.25	8.63	34.50
7.0 cfm + PS3 gun	41.40	31.63	15.81	63.25
7.0 cfm + PS3 gun + pressure container	51.18	39.10	19.55	78.20
Airless spray				
heavy duty	80.50	60.38	30.19	120.75
Compressors				
Portable 2.5 cfm, electric	16.10	12.08	6.04	24.15
Industrial 7 cfm, electric	34.50	26.45	13.23	52.90
Industrial 15 cfm, electric/petrol	43.70	32.78	16.39	65.55

	4 hrs or 5–9am £	First 24 hrs £	Addit. 24 hrs £	Per week £
Spray guns				
Pressure feed gun	6.90	5.18	2.59	10.35
Syphon cup gun 1 litre	6.90	5.18	2.59	10.35
Gravity feed hopper gun	9.78	7.48	3.74	14.95
Pressure feed containers 12.5/22.5 litre	9.78	7.48	3.74	14.95

	First 24 hrs £	Addit. 24 hrs £	Per week £
Lifting/materials handling			
Mini excavator/digger	85.10	42.55	170.20
Rubbish chute, per 1 m section	2.99	1.50	5.98
Winching			
Tirfor			
1600 kg	13.50	7.76	31.05
3200 kg	19.55	9.78	39.10
Gin wheel	–	–	5.75
Fall rope			
50′	–	–	4.60
100′	–	–	6.90
Panel lifting winch	14.95	7.48	29.90
Hoisting			
Scaffold hoist, electric, 150 kg	31.63	15.81	63.25
Roof tile hoist	85.10	42.55	170.20
Chain hoist			
10 cwt (500 kg)	10.93	5.46	21.85
20 cwt (1000 kg)	12.08	6.04	24.15
30/40 cwt (1500/2000 kg)	14.38	7.19	28.75

	Weekend rate £	First 24 hrs £	Addit. 24 hrs £	Per week £
Gardening equipment				
Hedge trimmers				
petrol engine	18.40	12.08	12.08	36.80
electric	9.20	6.33	6.33	18.40
Cultivators				
5.0 hp digger	27.60	18.40	18.40	59.80
Medium duty rotovator	44.85	29.90	29.90	109.25
Heavy duty rotovator	55.20	36.80	36.80	120.75
Mowers				
18″ rotary, petrol	14.95	9.78	9.78	36.80
28″ rotary, petrol	55.20	36.80	36.80	110.40
36″ powered, scythe	55.20	36.80	36.80	110.40
Powered brush cutter	21.85	14.38	14.38	50.60
Flame gun, gas operated	6.90	4.60	4.60	13.80
Ride-on mower	72.45	48.30	48.30	144.90
Lawn care				
Powered scarifier/thatcher	27.60	18.40	18.40	55.20
Manual aerator	4.60	2.88	2.88	8.63
Powered aerator	27.60	18.40	18.40	55.20
Lawn rake, electric	8.63	5.75	5.75	17.25
Lawn edger	8.63	5.75	5.75	17.25
Tree stump, chipper	36.80	24.73	24.73	74.75
Log splitter, hydraulic	23.00	15.53	15.53	46.00
Post hole borers				
Powered earth drill, 7″/9″	36.80	24.73	24.73	74.75
Powered auger, 3″/5″	25.88	17.25	17.25	48.30
Manual post hole borer, 6″/9″	4.60	2.88	2.88	8.63

	Weekend rate £	First 24 hrs £	Addit. 24 hrs £	Per week £
General gardening tools				
Axe 36″ felling	–	–	–	3.45
Bow saw, crosscut saw, 2 man	–	–	–	3.45
Fork/spade	–	–	–	3.45
Garden roller	–	3.45	1.73	6.90
Insecticide spray	–	4.60	2.30	9.20
Scythe	–	–	–	3.45
Shears-lawn/edging/tree lopping	–	–	–	3.45
Wheel barrow	–	3.45	1.73	6.90
Turfing iron	–	–	–	3.45

WIRING & INSTALLING
LAMPS
CEILING
TILING
TO INSTALLING HOOD
DOUBLE GLAZING
CUPBOARDS
CUPBOARDS INSTALLING
TILING

6 Total project costs

This chapter lists the approximate costs of complete items of work, e.g. conservatories, swimming pools. The cost of the supply of the materials is stated together with the cost of the erection where it is carried out by a contractor. The comments made at the end of Chapter 2 about the relationship between the cost of this type of improvement and the increased value of the property should be studied carefully. Briefly, it is only worth having swimming pools, sun lounges and conservatories built if you are going to enjoy the facility yourself because it is unlikely you will be able to recover the whole of the capital cost on the sale of the house.

Extensions

Building an extension to your home can be the easiest way of creating more living space without the harassment of moving. It is difficult to produce accurate square foot prices for the cost of construction because of wide variations in the quality of materials available. However, for a brick built, flat roof extension constructed in traditional materials a guide figure of £45 to £50 per square foot could be used. This is based upon the most popular size extension of 12′ × 8′ and the figures quoted would increase per square foot if the area was smaller and decrease if the area was larger.

If the extension is two storey you should add the areas of both floors together to make the calculation.

Conservatories and sun lounges

The following cost information is based upon information kindly supplied by Banbury Homes and Gardens Ltd, P.O. Box 17, Banbury, Oxfordshire, OX17 3NS and you should write for their catalogue in order to identify the various types available. The prices are current at the time of writing and include VAT.

	Supplied only £	Supplied and erected £
Sovereign		
6′3″ × 8′4″	799.00	939.00
6′3″ × 10′4″	899.00	1049.00
6′3″ × 12′5″	1005.00	1165.00
8′3″ × 8′4″	919.00	1215.00
8′3″ × 10′4″	1035.00	1349.00
8′3″ × 12′5″	1145.00	1479.00
Sovereign de luxe		
6′3″ × 8′4″	839.00	989.00
6′3″ × 10′4″	939.00	1099.00
6′3″ × 12′5″	1045.00	1215.00
8′3″ × 8′4″	1055.00	1215.00
8′3″ × 10′4″	1179.00	1349.00
8′3″ × 12′5″	1299.00	1479.00
New leisure room		
6′5″ × 8′4″	1178.00	1304.00
6′5″ × 10′5″	1294.00	1429.00
8′5″ × 8′4″	1494.00	1640.00
8′5″ × 10′5″	1650.00	1822.00
Garden lounge		
7′7″ × 9′11″	1449.00	1695.00
7′7′ × 12′4″	1649.00	1895.00
7′7′ × 14′10″	1849.00	2105.00
Laser		
7′6″ × 10′0″	1899.00	2135.00
7′6″ × 12′6″	1999.00	2245.00
7′6″ × 14′11″	2099.00	2355.00

	Supplied only £	Supplied and erected £
Elan (white finish)		
8′3″ × 10′5″	1820.00	1985.00
8′3″ × 12′6″	1930.00	2105.00
8′3″ × 14′6″	2123.00	2315.00
8′3″ × 16′6″	2361.00	2566.00
8′3″ × 18′6″	2658.00	2878.00
8′3″ × 20′6″	2943.00	3178.00
10′3″ × 10′5″	2123.00	2298.00
10′3″ × 12′6″	2382.00	2492.00
10′3″ × 14′6″	2524.00	2729.00
10′3″ × 16′6″	2704.00	2924.00
10′3″ × 18′6″	3035.00	3273.00
10′3″ × 20′6″	3313.00	3563.00
Galaxie (double glazed with clear or tinted polycarbonate roof)		
8′4″ × 10′10″	4353.00	4610.00
8′4″ × 12′10″	4764.00	5045.00
8′4″ × 14′11″	5169.00	5475.00
8′4″ × 17′0″	5575.00	5905.00
8′4″ × 19′0″	5979.00	6345.00
8′4″ × 21′1″	6565.00	6955.00
10′3″ × 10′10″	4655.00	4930.00
10′3″ × 12′10″	5110.00	5410.00
10′3″ × 14′11″	5550.00	5875.00
10′3″ × 17′0″	5982.00	6330.00
10′3″ × 19′0″	6426.00	6810.00
10′3″ × 21′1″	6857.00	7265.00
11′9″ × 10′10″	4892.00	5185.00
11′9″ × 12′10″	5362.00	5680.00
11′9″ × 14′11″	5833.00	6175.00
11′9″ × 17′0″	6303.00	6670.00
11′9″ × 19′0″	6773.00	7175.00
11′9″ × 21′1″	7329.00	7855.00
14′0″ × 10′10″	5913.00	6225.00
14′0″ × 12′10″	6489.00	6825.00
14′0″ × 14′11″	6994.00	7355.00
14′0″ × 17′0″	7635.00	8020.00
14′0″ × 19′0″	8215.00	8635.00
14′0″ × 21′1″	9010.00	9455.00

	Supplied only £	Supplied and erected £
Corniche (clear polycarbonate roof)		
8′9″ × 10′7″	4555.00	4765.00
8′9″ × 13′2″	5020.00	5225.00
8′9″ × 15′8″	5525.00	5725.00
8′9″ × 18′3″	6050.00	6245.00
8′9″ × 20′10″	6645.00	6835.00
11′6″ × 10′7″	5590.00	5745.00
11′6″ × 13′2″	6150.00	6345.00
11′6″ × 15′8″	6762.00	6945.00
11′6″ × 18′3″	7390.00	7565.00
11′6″ × 20′10″	8045.00	8205.00
Tropique (brown finish)		
8′3″ × 10′5″	2510.00	2800.00
8′3″ × 12′6″	2749.00	3059.00
8′3″ × 14′6″	2989.00	3319.00
8′3″ × 16′6″	3136.00	3586.00
8′3″ × 18′6″	3587.00	3957.00
8′3″ × 20′9″	3933.00	4323.00
10′3″ × 10′5″	2852.00	3162.00
10′3″ × 12′6″	3084.00	3414.00
10′3″ × 14′6″	3403.00	3753.00
10′3″ × 16′6″	3728.00	4098.00
10′3″ × 18′6″	3964.00	4354.00
10′3″ × 20′7″	4295.00	4705.00
Sunbury		
6′0″ × 6′1″	920.00	1144.00
6′0″ × 8′2″	1095.00	1370.00
6′0″ × 9′11″	1150.00	1469.00
6′0″ × 11′10″	1255.00	1590.00
6′0″ × 13′9″	1365.00	1777.00
6′0″ × 15′8″	1460.00	1920.00
6′0″ × 17′7″	1560.00	2063.00

	Supplied only £	Supplied and erected £
Mistral (white finish)		
8′6″ × 10′6″	2124.00	2324.00
8′6″ × 12′6″	2234.00	2444.00
8′6″ × 14′6″	2371.00	2596.00
8′6″ × 16′6″	2542.00	2787.00
8′6″ × 18′7″	2896.00	3161.00
8′6″ × 20′7″	3128.00	3408.00
10′6″ × 10′6″	2414.00	2624.00
10′6″ × 12′6″	2611.00	2836.00
10′6″ × 14′6″	2791.00	3036.00
10′6″ × 16′6″	2939.00	3199.00
10′6″ × 18′7″	3192.00	3472.00
10′6″ × 20′7″	3561.00	3861.00

All the above conservatories need to be erected on a concrete base. If the work is carried out by a builder it should cost you approximately £45 per square yard for conservatory bases and £30–£35 for garage and greenhouse bases. If you do it yourself the material costs should be about £18 per square yard for conservatory bases and £15 for garage and greenhouse bases and to lay the base it should take you approximately 3 hours per square yard. All these figures assume there are no complications with existing drains or services or any other obstructions situated on the site of the proposed building.

Garages

The types of garages quoted here are supplied by Banbury Homes and Gardens Ltd, P.O. Box 17, Banbury, Oxfordshire, OX17 3NS. All the prices given refer to 'textured brick finish' appearance to the panels. The comments made earlier in the conservatory section about concrete bases also applies here.

	Supplied only £	Supplied and erected £
The Kent		
14′6″ × 8′10″	1174.00	1341.00
18′4″ × 8′10″	1408.00	1604.00
22′2″ × 8′10″	1553.00	1781.00
The Sussex		
16′5″ × 8′10″	1297.00	1478.00
18′4″ × 8′10″	1420.00	1616.00
20′3″ × 8′10″	1479.00	1687.00
The Norfolk		
16′5″ × 9′9″	1364.00	1560.00
18′4″ × 9′9″	1475.00	1684.00
20′3″ × 9′9″	1541.00	1769.00
The Dorset		
16′5″ × 10′9″	1464.00	1673.00
18′4″ × 10′9″	1591.00	1819.00
20′3″ × 10′9″	1657.00	1902.00
The Oxford		
16′5″ × 14′7″	2032.00	2358.00
18′4″ × 14′7″	2209.00	2557.00
20′3″ × 14′7″	2310.00	2683.00
The Cambridge		
16′5″ × 16′6″	2237.00	2563.00
18′4″ × 16′6″	2436.00	2784.00
20′3″ × 16′6″	2543.00	2916.00
The Somerset		
16′5″ × 18′3″	2821.00	3288.00
18′4″ × 18′3″	3021.00	3529.00
22′2″ × 18′3″	3159.00	3702.00

Greenhouses

The following is based upon information supplied by Banbury Homes and Gardens Ltd and covers two types of aluminium greenhouses – freestanding and lean-to. The comments made earlier in the conservatory section about concrete bases apply here.

	Supplied only £	Supplied and erected £
Free standing aluminium greenhouse		
6′ × 6′	225.00	No erection services supplied
6′ × 8′	242.00	
8′ × 10′	355.00	
8′ × 12′	382.00	
8′ × 10′ Euro	439.00	
8′ × 12′ Euro	495.00	
Lean-to aluminium greenhouse		
6′ × 10′	360.00	As above
6′ × 12′	399.00	
Free standing cedar greenhouse 'Amateur' range		
6′5″ × 8′0″	565.00	655.00
6′5″ × 10′6″	640.00	740.00
8′0″ × 8′0″	620.00	720.00
8′0″ × 10′6″	715.00	825.00
8′0″ × 13′0″	810.00	930.00
8′0″ × 15′7″	910.00	1040.00
10′0″ × 10′6″	780.00	895.00
10′0″ × 13′0″	885.00	1010.00
10′0″ × 15′7″	995.00	1130.00
10′0″ × 18′0″	1100.00	1245.00
10′0″ × 20′7″	1210.00	1365.00
Lean-to cedar greenhouse 'Amateur' range		
7′0″ × 8′0″	485.00	585.00
7′0″ × 10′6″	550.00	660.00
7′0″ × 13′0″	615.00	735.00
7′0″ × 15′7″	680.00	810.00
7′0″ × 18′0″	740.00	880.00
7′0″ × 20′7″	805.00	955.00

	Supplied only £	Supplied and erected £
Free standing cedar greenhouse		
'Traditional' range		
6′5″ × 5′6″	470.00	590.00
6′5″ × 8′0″	540.00	630.00
7′7″ × 10′6″	715.00	825.00
7′7″ × 13′0″	815.00	935.00
10′0″ × 13′0″	885.00	1010.00
Lean-to cedar greenhouse		
'Traditional' range		
5′0″ × 5′5″	425.00	525.00
5′0″ × 10′6″	480.00	590.00
5′0″ × 13′0″	530.00	650.00

Swimming pools

The information on outdoor pools is based on the products of Penguin Swimming Pools Ltd, Baker Lane, Galleywood, Chelmsford, Essex. Their Penguin range of domestic pools can be supplied in kit form which includes everything except ready mix concrete, the excavation itself and some small items of materials which can be purchased locally. The 'Royal', the 'King' and the 'Emperor' pools can be constructed in any size or shape and cost approximately 10% more than the standard rectangular pool. There are many extra items available and you should write to the above address for further information.

	Supplied only £	Supplied and erected £
'Little Blue' pool		
6 × 3 m	3100.00	7950.00
7 × 3.5 m	3350.00	8800.00
8 × 4 m	3700.00	9700.00
9 × 4.5 m	4000.00	10850.00
10 × 5 m	4350.00	11450.00
'Royal' pool		
6 × 3 m	3650.00	9650.00
7 × 3.5 m	3950.00	10200.00
8 × 4 m	4250.00	11350.00
9 × 4.5 m	4700.00	12950.00
10 × 5 m	5050.00	14700.00
12 × 6 m	6050.00	16550.00
'King' pool		
6 × 3 m	3850.00	10350.00
7 × 3.5 m	4350.00	11500.00
8 × 4 m	4650.00	12800.00
9 × 4.5 m	5150.00	14550.00
10 × 5 m	5650.00	16550.00
12 × 6 m	6700.00	18700.00

	Supplied only £	Supplied and erected £
'Emperor' pool		
6 × 3 m	6650.00	15500.00
7 × 3.5 m	7200.00	16550.00
8 × 4 m	7950.00	18400.00
9 × 4.5 m	9050.00	20400.00
10 × 5 m	9700.00	23300.00
12 × 6 m	11250.00	26650.00

You should also allow for delivery charges which vary from approximately £50 to £500 depending upon the distance to your home from Essex.

Loft conversions

Converting your loft to provide extra floor space is a popular method of increasing accommodation and is less expensive than building an extension at ground floor level. If you are considering this course of action you must give careful thought to the question of access.

It is pointless to spend a lot of money on the conversion if the access to it is by ladder! A proper extension needs a staircase and finding room at first floor level is not easy in a normal size house. There are of course many patent ladder systems on the market which fold away when not in use but these are only really suitable if the loft is going to be used occasionally for say a store or for a model railway layout.

It is difficult to provide costs of this type of work but £7000 to £9000 could be taken as indicative of what a contractor would charge for converting the loft of an average sized semi-detached house. This includes a new floor, lining the roof, a new access staircase and 2 dormer windows.

ROOM
12 ft x 15 ft
1 foot = ·3048 metres
1 LITRE = ·22 Gallons
? Pints
Sandpaper
WALLPAPER 1'9" 54 cms
3 ROLLS WALLPAPER
4 5
4 Brushes
2 Rollers
WHITE EMULSION
3 TINS
LITRES?
GLOSS Paint
Undercoat
3 Bottles Beer

7 General data

The following information is included to assist you in whatever calculation you need to make in the pursuit of your DIY activities.

Imperial and metric equivalents

Temperature

In order to convert Fahrenheit to Centigrade deduct 32 and multiply by 5/9. To convert Centigrade to Fahrenheit multiply by 9/5 and add 32.

Fahrenheit	Centigrade	Fahrenheit	Centigrade
230	110.0	110	43.3
220	104.4	90	32.2
210	98.9	80	26.7
200	93.3	70	21.1
190	87.8	60	15.6
180	82.2	50	10.0
170	76.7	40	4.4
160	71.1	30	– 1.1
150	65.6	20	– 6.7
140	60.0	10	– 12.2
130	54.4	0	– 17.8
120	48.9		

Length

Imperial		Metric	
12 inches	= 1 foot	10 millimetres	= 1 centimetre
3 feet	= 1 yard	100 centimetres	= 1 metre
22 yards	= 1 chain	1000 metres	= 1 kilometre
10 chains	= 1 furlong		
8 furlongs	= 1 mile		
6080 feet	= 1 nautical mile		
6 feet	= 1 fathom		

Area

Imperial		Metric	
4840 square yards	= 1 acre	10,000 square metres	= 1 hectare
640 acres	= 1 square mile		

Weight

Imperial		Metric	
16 ounces	= 1 pound	1000 grammes	= 1 kilogramme
14 pounds	= 1 stone	1000 kilogrammes	= 1 tonne
2 stones	= 1 quarter		
4 quarters	= 1 hundredweight		
20 hundredweights	= 1 ton		
1 cental	= 100 pounds		

Conversion

In order to convert Imperial measurements into metric, you should multiply by the factors shown below. You should divide by the same factors to change from metric to Imperial.

Length

			Factor
Miles	:	kilometres	1.60934
Yards	:	metres	0.9144
Feet	:	metres	0.3048
Inches	:	millimetres	25.4
Inches	:	centimetres	2.54

Imperial	Metric millimetre (mm)	Imperial	Metric millimetre (mm)
1¼″	31.8	9″	228.6
1½″	38.1	10″	254.0
1¾″	44.5	11″	279.4
2″	50.8	12″	304.8
2¼″	57.2	15″	381.0
2½″	63.5	16″	406.4
3″	76.2	18″	457.2
4″	101.6	21″	533.4
5″	127.0	24″	609.6
6″	152.4	27″	685.8
7″	177.8	36″	914.4
8″	203.2		

Imperial	Metric metre (m)	Imperial	Metric metre (m)
3′	0.914	17′	5.18*
4′	1.219	18′	5.485*
5′	1.524	19′	5.79*
6′	1.829	20′	6.095*
7′	2.135*	30′	9.145*
8′	2.44*	40′	12.19*
9′	2.745*	50′	15.24*
10′	3.05*	75′	22.86*
11′	3.35*	100′	30.48*
12′	3.66*	200′	60.96*
13′	3.96*	300′	91.44*
14′	4.27*	500′	152.4*
15′	4.57*	1000′	304.8*
16′	4.88*		

** to nearest 5 mm*

Area

Square miles	:	square kilometres	2.58999
Square miles	:	hectares	258.999
Acres	:	square metres	4046.86
Acres	:	hectares	0.404686
Square yards	:	square metres	0.836127
Square feet	:	square metres	0.092903
Square feet	:	square centimetres	929.03
Square inches	:	square millimetres	645.16
Square inches	:	square centimetres	6.4516

A full Conversion Table is provided on the inside cover.

Volume

Cubic yards	:	cubic metres	0.764555
Cubic feet	:	cubic metres	0.0283168
Cubic feet	:	cubic decimetres	28.3168
Cubic inches	:	cubic centimetres	16.3871

Weight

Tons	:	kilogrammes	1016.05
Tons	:	tonnes	1.01605
Hundredweights	:	kilogrammes	50.8023
Centals	:	kilogrammes	45.3592
Quarters	:	kilogrammes	12.7006
Stones	:	kilogrammes	6.35029
Pounds	:	kilogrammes	0.45359237
Ounces	:	grammes	28.3495

Average weights of materials

Material	tonnes per m^3
Ashes	0.68
Aluminium	2.68
Asphalt	2.31
Brickwork – engineering	2.24
Brickwork – common	1.86
Bricks – engineering	2.40
Bricks – common	2.00
Cement – Portland	1.45
Cement – rapid hardening	1.34
Clay – dry	1.05
Clay – wet	1.75
Coal	0.90
Concrete	2.30
Concrete – reinforced	2.40
Earth – topsoil	1.60
Glass	2.60
Granite – solid	2.70
Gravel	1.76
Iron	7.50
Lead	11.50
Limestone – crushed	1.75
Plaster	1.28
Sand	1.90
Slate	2.80
Tarmacadam	1.57
Timber – general construction	0.70
Water	1.00

DICTIONARY

Glossary

The following terms have been included to assist lay people in their DIY activities. If you come across other words or unfamiliar specialist terms, consult a good technical dictionary (e.g. *The Penguin Dictionary of Building*) or a do-it-yourself manual (e.g. *The Collins Complete Do-It-Yourself Manual*).

Accelerator	A chemical additive used to speed up the setting of mortar or concrete.
Acoustic plaster	Plaster with porous and/or textured surface to absorb sound.
Aggregate	The material which is usually the largest element in a concrete mix, e.g. stone or gravel.
Agricultural drain	Unglazed, unsocketed and unjointed pipe to drain sub-soil. Sometimes perforated on top surface to allow water to enter.
Anaglypta	A heavy, embossed wallpaper.
Architrave	A piece of timber covering the joint between a door or window frame and the plaster.
Auger	A corkscrew shaped tool used for drilling holes.
Back drop	A vertical pipe in a manhole connecting the branch to the invert pipe. It is used to save long lengths of unnecessary excavation.
Backfilling	The excavated material that is returned, filled and rammed around foundations.
Back putty	The narrow strip of putty between the inside face of the glass and the edge of the rebate.
Barge board	A sloping board fixed to the gable end of a roof.
Batten	A small section of non-structural timber.
Beam filling	Brickwork infilling between joists.
Benching	The arrangement of concrete in the bottom of a manhole at the sides of the main channel and branches.

Blinding	The top surface of hardcore or broken bricks filled with sand to provide a smooth surface to receive concrete.
Bloom	A film on gloss painted surfaces caused by defective workmanship or materials.
Bonding	The arrangement of bricks or blocks in a pattern to present an attractive appearance and provide structural strength, which is usually achieved by arranging the vertical joints in non-continuous lines.
Bradawl	Hand tool used for making holes in wood for screws.
Browning coat	The middle coat of plaster in three coat work.
Built up roofing	Two or three layers of bituminous roofing felt bedded in bitumen.
Butterfly wall tie	A wall tie made of galvanised wire formed into a double triangular shape.
Came	An 'H' shaped piece of lead to receive the glass in leaded windows.
Capillary joint	A joint in copper pipework made by placing a fitting over the end of a copper pipe which is marginally smaller than the fitting. The small space between the two is filled with molten solder to make the joint watertight.
Casement door	A fully glazed door.
Casement window	The opening part of a window.
Casing	The timber lining to a window or door opening.
Caulked joint	A joint where the jointing material (usually lead or asbestos rope) is pressed into place by a caulking tool.
Cavity wall	A form of constructing external walls in two leaves with a cavity between them. The leaves are tied by the building in of wall ties across the cavity.
Cement fillet	A triangular section of mortar at the junction of a vertical and horizontal surface to prevent water penetration.
Cement grout	A liquified mix of cement and water.
Close boarded fencing	Vertical softwood boards fixed to horizontal rails to form solid fence.
Comb	A toothed metal plate used for spreading adhesive or scratching plaster to receive the next coat.
Compression joint	A method of jointing copper pipework in which the pipe ends are connected by tightening up brass nuts which force glands into the walls of the pipes.

Conduit	A plastic or metal pipe to receive electric cables. It is used to provide easy renewal or repair of the cables without disturbing the plaster or concrete.
Coping	The course of bricks or concrete slab on the top of a wall.
Countersinking	A depression made so that the head of a screw can be driven flush with the surface of the material.
Curtain wall	The infilling to a frame which has no structural properties.
Dado	The lower part of an internal wall with two different finished surfaces.
Damp proof course	A layer of impervious material laid in walls to prevent the rising of moisture.
Decking	Horizontal rigid sheeting secured to joists as a floor or roof surface.
Dowel	A short round piece of hardwood or metal sunk into two separate members to strengthen the connection.
Dry lining	The system of using plasterboard or similar to form the surface of walls instead of wet plastering.
Dry walling	Walls where the stones are laid dry without the use of mortar.
Eaves	That part of the roof that projects beyond the face of the external wall.
Efflorescence	The unsightly deposit of crystallized salts on walls caused by the evaporation of water leaving the salt deposit on the surface. Can be removed by washing or brushing.
Elevation	A drawing showing the vertical face of a building.
Expansion pipe	An overflow pipe from a hot water cylinder discharging over the cold water tank in case of the water overheating.
Facing brick	A brick which is generally more attractive in appearance than common bricks and used mainly in external walls.
Fascia	A vertical timber board fixed to the end of rafters to receive rainwater gutter.
Fenestration	The arrangement of windows on a building elevation.
Field drain	*see* Agricultural drain.
Firring piece	Splayed piece of timber nailed to the top of roof joists to create the fall on a flat roof.

Flashing	A method of making the joint between a roof and wall watertight by inserting a strip of flexible metal or bitumen.
Flaunching	The cement mortar placed around chimney pots to deflect rainwater on to the roof.
Free standing	An element which is not supported by an adjacent structure.
Frustum	Lower part of cone whose top surface is parallel to the base.
Going	The width of the horizontal tread in a staircase. The total going is the sum of tread goings.
Granolithic concrete	A hard wearing concrete used for floor finishes. The aggregate used in the mix is selected to produce extra strength.
Hardcore	Broken brick or stones laid as a base to receive concrete beds.
Haunching	*see* Benching.
Header	A brick laid so that only the end is exposed.
Heave	A swelling of the clay caused by excess water which can cause movement in buildings.
Hollow wall	*see* Cavity wall.
Immersion heater	A single or double electric element fitted inside an insulated copper cylinder.
Inspection chamber	A shallow manhole position at junction of main drain and branches.
Interceptor trap	A trap set at the end of a drainage system between the main sewer and the drain to prevent the ingress of vermin and gases.
Jamb	The inside vertical face of an opening or the vertical side member of a window or door frame.
Jointing	The mortar placed between the vertical and horizontal faces of bricks.
Joist	A supporting beam in floors or roofs usually made of timber or steel.
Key	The scoring effect on a surface to assist the adhesion of a further coat.
Keying in	The bonding or joining of old and new brickwork.
Kicking plate	A metal plate screwed to the lower part of a door to prevent damage.
King post	A type of roof truss.

Latex screed	A screed applied in thin layers to existing concrete or screed to provide level surface for floor finish.
Lining paper	A thin paper pasted to walls or ceiling to conceal irregularities before papering or painting.
Lintol	A timber or steel structural member placed over a door or window opening to take the weight of the wall above.
Lost headed nail	A nail whose head is only slightly larger than the nail so that it can be driven below the surface of the timber.
Mansard roof	A roof where each side has two different angled slopes.
Marine plywood	Exterior quality plywood.
Masonry nail	A hardened nail that can be driven or fired into concrete or brickwork.
Mastic	A non-setting material used for sealing joists.
Mirror screw	A screw with a detachable dome head which is fixed after the screw has been secured.
Mono-pitched roof	A roof with only one sloping face.
Mortise	A recess cut in timber to receive tongue or tenon from another member.
Mullion	A vertical structural member of a window.
Muntin	A vertical member of a framed door.
Needle	A horizontal beam used in shoring.
Newel	A post in a staircase that supports the handrail.
Nogging	A short horizontal timber member between vertical studding in partition.
Open eaves	An arrangement where the soffit board is fixed between the projecting rafters so that the rafters are partially exposed.
Opening light	The part of a window that opens.
Oriel window	A window above ground floor level that projects beyond the face of the wall.
Pargetting	The rendering to a chimney flue.
Pebble dash	An external finish to walls produced by throwing pebbles on to rendering before it has set.
Pin kerb	A small precast concrete kerb usually 6″ × 2″ (150 × 50 mm) used mainly as path edging.
Pointing	The operation of raking out the mortar between the bricks (*see* Jointing).
Purlin	A horizontal roof member which supports the rafters.

Raft foundation	A reinforced concrete slab with extra concrete at perimeter to form a ground beam. Used mainly in poor ground conditions.
Rag bolt	A bolt with an irregular shaped end, cast into concrete for greater strength.
Rebate	A rectangular recess cut into the edge of a timber member such as a window frame to form seating for glass.
Reconstructed stone	Precast concrete made by adding stone dust to the cement to produce a stone effect.
Reveal	Vertical face of opening.
Sash	*see* Opening light.
Sand blasting	A process of cleaning stone or brickwork by hosing it with high pressure water and sand.
Screed	A layer of material laid on concrete to provide smooth surface to receive finishing material.
Scrimmed and filled joint	A technique of concealing plasterboard joints by filling with cloth and applying a thin coat of plaster.
Sett	Stone block used for decorative paving.
Sharp sand	Used in mixing concrete.
Soakaway	A stone filled pit to receive surface water.
Soffit board	Horizontal board secured to underside of rafters under overhanging eaves.
Soft sand	Used in mixing mortar.
Spur	A branch from a ring main usually for a new socket outlet.
Stucco	Smooth external rendering.
Studding	Timber framed partition.
Sump	A pit below floor level.
Tanking	A vertical and horizontal waterproofed membrane to prevent the ingress of water.
Taped and filled joint	A technique of concealing joints between paper tape in lieu of cloth prior to plastering. (*see* Scrimmed and filled joint.)
Template	A full size pattern used for cutting round to produce required profile of permanent material.
Tile hanging	The vertical fixing of roofing tiles.
Uncoursed	The arrangement of irregular stones in a wall without a continuous horizontal bed.

Underpinning	The technique of replacing a load bearing wall below ground level by providing temporary supports in short lengths whilst the new wall and foundation is constructed.
Upstand	A vertical flashing usually at junction of horizontal and vertical surfaces.
Vapour barrier	A layer of impermeable material to prevent the penetration of moist air.
Verge	The edge of a sloping roof at the gables.
Wall plate	A horizontal timber member set on top of wall to receive rafters or joists.
Wall tie	A piece of twisted metal built into each leaf of a cavity wall.

Index

Metric/Imperial area conversion table

Imperial dimension (ft)	Square feet	Square yards	Square metres	Metric dimension (mm)	Metric dimension (m)
3′ × 5′	15	1.66	1.39	914 × 1524	0.91 × 1.52
3′ × 6′	18	2.00	1.67	914 × 1829	0.91 × 1.83
3′ × 7′	21	2.33	1.95	914 × 2134	0.91 × 2.13
3′ × 8′	24	2.67	2.23	914 × 2438	0.91 × 2.44
3′ × 9′	27	3.00	2.51	914 × 2743	0.91 × 2.74
3′ × 10′	30	3.34	2.79	914 × 3048	0.91 × 3.05
4′ × 5′	20	2.22	1.86	1219 × 1524	1.22 × 1.52
4′ × 6′	24	2.67	2.23	1219 × 1829	1.22 × 1.83
4′ × 7′	28	3.11	2.60	1219 × 2134	1.22 × 2.13
4′ × 8′	32	3.55	2.97	1219 × 2438	1.22 × 2.44
4′ × 9′	36	3.99	3.34	1219 × 2743	1.22 × 2.74
4′ × 10′	40	4.45	3.72	1219 × 3048	1.22 × 3.05
5′ × 5′	25	2.77	2.32	1524 × 1524	1.52 × 1.52
5′ × 6′	30	3.34	2.79	1524 × 1829	1.52 × 1.83
5′ × 7′	35	3.89	3.25	1524 × 2134	1.52 × 2.13
5′ × 8′	40	4.45	3.72	1524 × 2438	1.52 × 2.44
5′ × 9′	45	5.00	4.18	1524 × 2743	1.52 × 2.74
5′ × 10′	50	5.56	4.65	1524 × 3048	1.52 × 3.05
6′ × 6′	36	3.99	3.34	1829 × 1829	1.83 × 1.83
6′ × 7′	42	4.66	3.90	1829 × 2134	1.83 × 2.13
6′ × 8′	48	5.33	4.46	1829 × 2438	1.83 × 2.44
6′ × 9′	54	6.00	5.02	1829 × 2743	1.83 × 2.74
6′ × 10′	60	6.66	5.57	1829 × 3048	1.83 × 3.05
6′ × 11′	66	7.33	6.13	1829 × 3353	1.83 × 3.35
6′ × 12′	72	8.00	6.69	1829 × 3658	1.83 × 3.66
7′ × 7′	49	5.44	4.55	2134 × 2134	2.13 × 2.13
7′ × 8′	56	6.22	5.20	2134 × 2438	2.13 × 2.44
7′ × 9′	63	7.00	5.85	2134 × 2743	2.13 × 2.74
7′ × 10′	70	7.77	6.50	2134 × 3048	2.13 × 3.05
7′ × 11′	77	8.55	7.15	2134 × 3353	2.13 × 3.35
7′ × 12′	84	9.33	7.80	2134 × 3658	2.13 × 3.66
8′ × 8′	64	7.12	5.95	2438 × 2438	2.44 × 2.44
8′ × 9′	72	8.00	6.69	2438 × 2743	2.44 × 2.74
8′ × 10′	80	8.89	7.43	2438 × 3048	2.44 × 3.05
8′ × 11′	88	9.78	8.18	2438 × 3353	2.44 × 3.35
8′ × 12′	96	10.67	8.92	2438 × 3658	2.44 × 3.66
9′ × 9′	81	9.01	7.53	2743 × 2743	2.74 × 2.74
9′ × 10′	90	10.00	8.36	2743 × 3048	2.74 × 3.05
9′ × 11′	99	11.00	9.20	2743 × 3353	2.74 × 3.35
9′ × 12′	108	12.00	10.03	2743 × 3658	2.74 × 3.66